Wildlife Conservation in India-1

I0420918

ROAD TO NOWHERE

By

H.S. Pabla

First Edition: 2015

Second Edition: 2018

ISBN: 9781517097776

Publisher: HS Pabla

Printed by: Kindle Direct Publishing

Cover Design by: Alaya (Bulgaria)

Available from Amazon.in and Other Retail Outlets

(E-book Edition, in all e-formats, also Available from
Amazon.in, Smashwords.com, and Other E-retailers)

This book is dedicated to generations of Indian forest guards who have preserved India's forests and wildlife in the face of devastating pressures to consume it all.

Table of Contents

List of Abbreviations

CAMPFIRE	Communal Areas Management Programme for Indigenous Resources
CB	Census Bureau of USA
CWLW	Chief Wild Life Warden
FCA	Forest (Conservation) Act, 1980.
FRA	Tribals and Other Forest Dwellers (Recognition of Forest Rights) Act, 2006. (Popularly called the Forest Rights Act).
GDP	Gross Domestic Product
GoI	Government of India
IAFWA	International Association of Fish and Wildlife Management Agencies
IFA	Indian Forest Act, 1927
IUCN	International Union for Conservation of Nature and Natural Resources
MoEFCC	Ministry of Environment, Forest and Climate Change
MP	Madhya Pradesh
NBWL	National Board for Wildlife
NTCA	National Tiger Conservation Authority
PAs	Protected Areas
SBWL	State Board for Wildlife
TR	Tiger Reserve
$	US Dollar
USFWS	US Fish and Wildlife Service
WII	Wildlife Institute of India
WLPA	Wild Life (Protection) Act, 1972

Preface

Contrary to popular cynicism, people in government, like other citizens, also work with commitment and conviction. Apart from narrowly doing just what his job requires, a public servant often has a private commitment to some higher goal related to the domain he is working in or for. This is especially so in the forest service where you always feel responsible for preserving God's creation, apart from meeting the immediate goals of your office. The forest laws, which are meant to show the way how forests and wildlife are to be preserved, are the bible to a new recruit, and his conscience is clear as long as he feels that he is implementing the laws to the best of his ability.

When I first read the Indian Forest Act, 1927 (IFA) and the Wild Life (Protection) Act, 1972, (WLPA) they seemed to be so comprehensive yet simple that I never thought I would need any other tool to do my job. The IFA has remained virtually unaltered nearly 90 years of its existence, except some minor tinkering by the states. Despite the clamour by the rabble rousers to dump this colonial law, no one has been able to suggest a well-reasoned alternative. However, the WLPA has been amended so many times in its short life of only about 40 years that it is almost impossible to say that it is the same law which was enacted in 1972. And with every amendment, it became more and more difficult for me to live up to that solemn commitment that every forester makes to his profession on his first walk or drive in the forest under his care.

I cut my teeth in an environment in which hunting of wild animals was already a sin, although many of the prominent conservationists of those days were former sinners who were, presumably, trying to cleanse themselves. Although they must have hunted wildlife legally, whenever they did it, the common refrain for them was "these former poachers". The WLPA, the first ever comprehensive wildlife law that India has given itself, was primarily crafted under the influence of these luminaries. The original Act was so beautifully written that it could have lived as such forever, like the IFA. While defining the general direction in which the conservation vanguard was to move in future, it provided for site-specific flexibility, which is vital for a country as diverse as India. The overall scheme of the law was that under the watchful eye of the Centre, states were responsible for deciding how to conserve their wildlife. The Chief Wildlife Warden (CWLW) of the state was virtually the CEO of conservation in the state. But over time all the powers of the states were taken away through multiple amendments. As a result, the states now have virtually no control over their natural resources — particularly wildlife — and consequently, no feeling of ownership. States can designate protected areas but, once done, they need the Centre's permission to modify their boundaries even marginally. Even a blackbuck, which is a widespread crop pest, cannot be killed or captured by the states without the Centre's permission. Management plans of tiger reserves are no longer approved by the CWLW of the state. While the CWLW can allow people to enter parks for tourism, the Centre decides what kinds of tourism shall be allowed. The Centre, through the National Tiger Conservation Authority (NTCA), can give directions to any "person officer or authority" regarding tiger conservation and any violation of these directions is punishable with imprisonment. The list of such provisions is long. Interestingly, the states have never protested their neutering.

Although the curbing of the states' power to manage their wildlife was bad enough, the situation of the field officers became even worse. They need the support and guidance of the CWLW on many issues on a regular basis. The CWLW or the State Government are powerless to guide them, as they themselves require the approval of half a dozen bodies to be able to do anything significant in the state. For example, a park director will require the permission of the CWLW, the State Government, the State Board for Wildlife, the Ministry of Environment and Forests, the National Board for Wildlife and the NTCA before he can, say, move a tiger from one place to another. As a result of such crazy amendments, the law which was meant to strengthen conservation of wildlife became a hindrance.

As long as I was a field officer, I never thought there was a problem with our laws and continued to implement them with gusto. But when I came into supposedly more powerful positions, by virtue of my seniority, I started feeling stifled. Rather than using the law to do important things, I needed to find chinks in the law to move forward. When the Government of India started directing the states that people should not be allowed to see wildlife in protected areas, it became totally flabbergasting. Hunting was already banned in India, now tourism was also being banned. It brought to fore my yearning for an answer to a longstanding question: Why preserve dangerous wild animals if you cannot even see them, forget hunting?

The genesis of this book is this quest for an answer to this question which, surprisingly, no one in India asks. It is an effort to build justification for preserving wild animals which will otherwise be wiped out in conflict with immediate human needs. It is also an effort to comfort the conscience of the forester whose effort to save wild animals heaps misery on the poor forest neighbours. If we can make wild animals the source of rural livelihoods, the damage caused by animals can be accepted as a minor collateral damage. Unless that happens, conservation is only about buying time for the animals some of us love but many dread.

Jim Corbett was dead right when he pronounced that "when he (tiger) is exterminated, as he will be unless public opinion rallies to his support, India will be poorer by having lost the finest of its fauna", but he little knew that tiger can also be a bread winner as well. The public opinion will save tiger only if his role as a bread winner is recognised and encouraged. Let us make tiger an integral part of India's growth story.

In being able to put down these thoughts, I owe a huge debt to all my former colleagues in the Madhya Pradesh Forest department, the Wildlife Institute of India, and wherever I have travelled, who taught me my craft and helped me become what I am.

Harbhajan Singh Pabla
Bhopal, India.
August, 2015.

1

Introduction

This book is a critical review by an insider of the founding philosophy of, and future vision for, the conservation of wildlife in India. I spent 35 years in the Indian Forest Service, managing national parks and implementing the conservation policies of the country, and have had a ringside view of what has happened on the ground during this period. Seeing an incessant decline in the status of most species over such a long time made me wonder whether our approach to conservation is fundamentally sound or not. The thoughts that came to my mind are presented in this book. We have a lot of books with fancy pictures of tigers and elephants, but perhaps no work has examined the very fundamentals of conservation in India in any depth. Therefore, this book is completely different from what a usual book on Indian natural history is expected to be.

Although to the academia "wild life", more fashionably spelt as "wildlife" these days, means all living things that do not need human care on a day to day basis, the scope of the word in this book is limited to what common man calls wild life, i.e. the large mammals inhabiting our forests. Despite some odd good news here and there, the entire world is conscious of the fact that Indian wildlife is declining rather quickly and that our efforts to preserve this heritage are not bearing any fruit beyond buying time.

We all believe that preservation of wild animals is necessary for the well-being of the people of India. In fact, it is difficult to find a human being who does not support preservation of wildlife per se, although he may or may not have adequate reasons to back his opinion. I am not sure even I had a clear idea why we should preserve wildlife until quite late in life, although I was in the business of saving wildlife. I remember asking Mr. H.S. Panwar, the doyen of Indian wildlife management who was Director of Kanha National Park, on the day I completed my one-month training attachment with the park in 1980, to give me a lecture on "why save wildlife". He gave me all the usual moral and ecological reasons for preserving wildlife, and I myself have kept dispensing the same stuff all my life whenever opportunities came my way. Life continued at the same even pace in the righteous belief that we, the people in the business of conservation, were doing a great job of saving the world by saving wildlife, despite the fact that most of the country, except a few protected areas, had been cleared of all wildlife. Although I was surrounded by the well-known clamour for more stringent laws and their more effective enforcement to protect wildlife, somewhere on the way I started suspecting that, perhaps, something was more fundamentally wrong with our conservation policies and programmes than just the shortage of legal and administrative firepower. As I continued to ponder over the problem of disappearing wildlife, this feeling continued to grow stronger and stronger.

One day in 1997, while writing a piece for a local NGO"s magazine, the diagnosis dawned on me. It struck me that the argument that we were saving wildlife for the benefit of the people of India was totally hollow and farcical. We were — and are, in fact — saving our wildlife just for the emotional and moral satisfaction of a small, sophisticated, mainly urban minority, at the cost of a vast rural majority whose crops, livestock, and occasionally children, these animals eat (Pabla 1997). It occurred to me that, strangely, we were expecting the very people to spare and save wildlife who suffer extreme losses and hardships because of wild animals and because of the programmes aimed at preserving them for posterity. This is not the way to save wildlife, I thought.

The usual justification for saving dangerous wild animals is that in doing this we will be saving our forests that house our biodiversity and provide clean air, water and other goods for our survival. We little realise that forests can be saved for their own sake as they give so much to us, particularly the local people. These big mammals perform no ecological role except eating other animals or vegetation, which human beings can themselves do and profit from. Justifying the preservation of forests for producing dangerous animals, that destroy people's lives and livelihoods, amounts to arguing against forest conservation itself. If wild animals were to bring some economic benefits to the people, it would be an entirely different matter. Under the current conservation paradigm, local people have no way of benefiting from wildlife, as we do not manage wildlife as a natural resource for human welfare. People are not allowed to own, use or trade wild animals or their derivatives. Wildlife tourism, which can still generate significant economic benefits for locals, is only reluctantly tolerated (NTCA 2012).

While the environmental benefits of conservation are enjoyed by the entire society, the cost is borne only by the poorest people who inhabit our forested landscapes. Why would anyone help preserve tigers, leopards or elephants knowing very well that someday they may kill him, his children, or his livestock or may destroy his house or crops? People are not even free to protect themselves against these attacks, as the killing of wild animals is prohibited by law except with permission, which is virtually impossible to get and exorbitantly expensive to execute. Protection of crops against wild animals by non-lethal means is extremely expensive as it takes nearly 200 days of watch and ward, day and night, in the worst of weather. If, by any chance, conservation succeeds and the number of wild animals grows, the losses incurred by the local people and the dangers to their lives will also mount. Why would they allow that to happen? Illegally killing animals to protect crops is remunerative as the proceeds can be consumed, sold or shared with others, while hunting them with a permit is expensive as the quarry has to be handed back to the authorities for burning or burial. As the common man is powerless to change the policies of the government, he does what he can, clandestinely or overtly, to undermine the policies that hurt him. So, he will poison tigers that kill his cows and will snare the deer and antelopes that come near his crops, despite the ban on hunting. Poachers who hunt wild animals for trade make people and their crops safer and are, therefore, welcome. The religious, cultural and ecological reasons we often cite in support of conservation of dangerous animals do not cut any ice with the people who bear the brunt of conservation. So, if millions are actively undermining our conservation programmes, we should not be surprised if conservation is not working.

Ever since I thought I recognised this conundrum, I have been wondering about ways of making conservation work for the benefit of the masses instead of taking a heavy toll on them. Looking around the world, I was able to find — thanks to the internet — that wildlife is safe primarily where it benefits the people, particularly local communities in poor and developing countries. The best models of community-based conservation come from the African continent where local communities earn substantial incomes from wildlife tourism, including hunting tourism. Since the advent of conservation programmes that generate economic benefits for communities, wildlife populations have grown several folds in Zimbabwe[1] (Western et al. 1994), Namibia (Weaver and Skyer, 2003), Tanzania, Uganda, Zambia (Lewis et al. undated), etc. Although it is a fact that conservation of wildlife is much more difficult in India because of our extremely high population density, Pakistan, which also has a high population density, has shown that even under similar circumstances highly endangered species like the *markhor* (Capra *falconeri*) can be brought back from the brink if stakes of the local communities are created in their conservation.

When it first occurred to me that the future of wildlife is largely linked to the benefits it can generate for the society through hunting and tourism, and not necessarily with the number of guns and guards deployed for its protection, the idea scared me. I wondered: How can I advocate the killing of animals as a means of conservation? Like everyone else, I too thought that hunting was against the Indian culture while tourism disturbed and harmed wildlife. In any case, hunting for consumption was not permitted in our law, while our national parks were already overcrowded with tourists. Therefore, it seemed there was not much scope for generating any more benefits from wildlife, even if one wanted to. However, I continued to ponder over the issue and, over time, realised that, despite the ultra-conservative law and seemingly overwhelmed national parks, it was still possible to experiment with these thoughts to some extent. After all, the law does allow hunting of animals which are a threat to human life and property (especially crops), and the parks seemed overcrowded only because we were confining visitors to safaris in very small tourism zones. Some chinks in the law seemed promising for limited exploitation!

I thought the provision to hunt crop-raiding animals could be used to develop community-based sport hunting models, though the scope was rather narrow. The influx of, and benefits from, tourism could be increased significantly by enlarging the tourism zones and promoting new low-impact activities like camping, trekking, bird watching, etc. in parks. While the first was a long term proposition and was only a subject for discussion to build a consensus on the approach, in view of its legal and moral undertones, I thought changing the way we were doing our wildlife tourism should be an easier thing to do. So, I cautiously started writing and speaking about the sport-hunting idea while waiting for the day I would move into the wildlife wing of the department to revamp the tourism business of the forest department. That was around the year 2000.

The community-based hunting idea was enthusiastically supported by virtually everyone who heard it, except the well-known conservationists of the country. Some of them appreciated the underlying strength of the proposal but did not want to stand for it openly in view of the potential risk to their public images. For some of them, I virtually became an enemy from being a close friend and ally. Out of the general public, the idea was opposed mainly by those for whom killing of any kind was anathema, irrespective of the context. Overall, the opposition came primarily from two angles: 1) that killing is against the Indian culture and traditions, and 2) that allowing legal hunting will lead to an increase in illegal hunting. While it is anybody's guess whether it is easier to regulate a legal profession or a banned activity (e.g. drinking), I examined the myth that hunting will hurt our cultural and religious feelings in some detail and learnt that hunting and consumption of wild animals had been part of Indian culture ever since India was first inhabited by humans. This discussion is available in the chapter entitled "Cultural Foundations of Conservation."

Irrespective of the moral or ecological connotations of hunting, rural people suffer significant crop damage at the hands of wild animals and spend huge amounts of time and money in crop protection. They expect the government to give them some solution and every legislature sees a large number of questions and motions on this issue. As a result, most states, including MP, allow the killing of wild pig and *nilgai* (blue bull), the commonest and most widely distributed crop pests, but nearly everywhere the permit system is so cumbersome that it is virtually impossible to kill an animal with a permit. The MP rules had a ridiculous provision that the crop raiding *nilgai* has to be killed in the same field which it is accused of damaging! So the *nilgai* had to wait to be killed while the farmer ran from pillar to post to procure a hunting permit and hire a gun owner to do the killing. The biggest irony is that even if one is able to kill an animal, it has to be burned or buried. As a result, the expenses of killing crop-raiding animals are much more than the value of the crops so saved. So, people keep killing these animals without permits and then eat and share the meat as well. As a result, these animals have no long term future.

Reflecting over the issue, it occurred to me that rather than allowing poaching by the locals to go on, it should be possible to change the game by introducing hunting of these animals by tourists, which would earn much more from an animal than just the meat value, and giving all the revenue to the communities. This will make them more tolerant of the losses and sympathetic to the animals.

Once while travelling abroad with the forest minister of Madhya Pradesh in 2002, I got a chance to discuss my philosophy of community-based conservation (hunting) with him. He got very excited about the idea and insisted that I frame the rules to implement it, although I was not working in the wildlife wing. The Chief Wild Life Warden (CWLW) of the state was dead against anything suggesting the killing of animals. But the minister was so insistent that I had to frame the rules, which the CWLW hated. As a result, the state came up with a watered down version of my proposal in the form of the wild boar hunting rules of 2004, which allowed hunting of crop-raiding wild pigs for a fee but kept silent on the question of whether the meat can be used or not, and there was no provision for the hunting fees going to the communities. The state did not touch the *nilgai* hunting rules at all. As a result, nothing changed on the ground.

When I came into the wildlife wing in 2005, I drafted new rules for introducing community-based hunting of crop-raiding species and proposed them to the government. Every forest minister since then, including a Jain, up until the day of my retirement, was enthusiastic about the idea but, somehow, could not take the matter to culmination. Many times, the minister or secretary changed when matters came close to conclusion and we had to begin the entire process of convincing the newcomers afresh. In most cases, ministers needed much less convincing than the bureaucrats, especially if they came with some religious beliefs against killing. The matter was ready to go to the cabinet twice, but something happened to derail it at the last minute. The last minister I worked with, Mr. Sartaj Singh, was so enthusiastic about this policy that he overruled all objections from two principal secretaries in succession. But, unfortunately, he happened to mention this "great idea of his" to the chief minister (CM) in a departmental review meeting. The CM, without applying his mind to the issue, said, "No, no. No killing." The forest minister said nothing to the CM, then or later. I tried to convince him to talk to the CM separately, but nothing happened. As my time was also coming to a close, and I had a full agenda for my last days in the government, I could not push him hard enough.

Incidentally, my entry into the office of the Chief Wild Life Warden (CWLW) of Madhya Pradesh, as his assistant, in 2005, almost coincided with the creation of the National Tiger Conservation Authority (NTCA) in 2006. NTCA has been given vast powers to interfere in the working of the CWLW, who was, till then, the final authority to decide how wildlife and protected areas (PAs) were to be managed in the states. Virtually from day one, the NTCA started sending *advisories*[2] to the states that tourism in the core areas of tiger reserves was unacceptable and that the states should start "phasing out" tourism from these areas. Apart from the fact that I disliked the very idea of the centre interfering in the working of the states, NTCA's model of conservation was beyond my comprehension. These guidelines were completely contrary to what we wanted to do in the state. So, while we continued to oppose

NTCA's advisories, we cautiously started expanding the tourism zones of the tiger reserves and the diversity of activities through which people could enjoy their visits to the parks. This was meant to attract and accommodate more visitors without increasing the potential adverse impact. We gradually raised the park fees, and our tourism revenues went up from less than INR 4 crores ($0.66 mn) per annum in 2006 to over INR 20 crores ($3.3 mn) in 2012. This money started helping us tide over shortages and delays in government funding, while a progressively increasing share went to the neighbouring communities as well. Meanwhile, several versions of the NTCA's guidelines on tourism in tiger reserves, all proposing unreasonable regulations, were rejected by the state and the relations between the NTCA and the CWLW MP became visibly tense. In fact, we had differences with the NTCA on many issues, particularly over issues like the loss and reintroduction of tigers in Panna and the reintroduction of gaur into Bandhavgarh, and tourism became another flashpoint.

Matters came to a head when in a public interest litigation in the MP High Court Jabalpur (Writ Petition no. 12351/2010, Ajay Dubey vs. NTCA and others) and later in the Supreme Court (SLP no. 21339/2011), which demanded a ban on tourism in protected areas, as per NTCA guidelines, the state and NTCA stood on opposite sides. While the High Court refused to stop tourism in tiger reserves, the Supreme Court, after a brief stay, directed the Government of India (GoI) and the NTCA to issue guidelines under which wildlife tourism could be continued. The NTCA first issued guidelines reiterating its existing stand that tourism shall be phased out of protected areas in due course. But, under huge public pressure, it had to change its stand. So, it came up with revised guidelines (NTCA 2012) which accepted the role of tourism in conservation and community well-being, but could not resist the urge to impose crippling restrictions on the way wildlife tourism shall be conducted. For example, now tourism cannot be allowed in more than 20% of the core area or the existing area, whichever is lower; increasing wildlife populations for the purpose of improving tourism is an offence. Only a miniscule number of visitors can be allowed into the parks if the carrying capacity is calculated as prescribed. These guidelines clearly demonstrate that the NTCA, i.e. GoI, hates wildlife tourism but had to allow it in this crippled form only under duress. Under the impact of these guidelines, tourism in many parks has gone down significantly, destroying thousands of jobs and hundreds of businesses, killing their concern for conservation of tigers in the process. Fortunately, I had retired by then; otherwise, I would have had to suffer many more sleepless nights trying to deal with this crazy situation.

India had already foregone the hunting option for benefitting the society from conservation and is now sending out signals that she is also not interested in tourism. As there is no other way of preserving dangerous and problematic species, except generating significant benefits for the people who suffer their depredations, conservation of wildlife in India is likely to become harder and harder as the competition between human beings and animals intensifies in the coming decades.

India has been obsessed with tigers for the last 45 years and has put a huge amount of resources toward their conservation. However, we have only failure to show for our efforts, primarily because we could not create the stakes of the common man in the tiger's survival. A tiger may be exciting to a tourist, but it is a clear and present danger to the local man. He may tolerate its presence in the name of God's will, but our efforts to preserve this dangerous animal just do not make sense to him. However, if a part of his family income were to come from saving tigers and other wildlife, and if more tigers bring him more income, conservation will make sense to him. The challenge, therefore, is to find ways of generating direct benefits from conservation for the local people through sustainable tourism.

The chapters named as "Wildlife Tourism: A Conservation Tool" and "Hunting for Conservation" discuss these issues in detail and show numerous examples where conservation and people benefit from each other through viewing (photographic) tourism and hunting tourism.

An important issue in conservation is the law that directs and regulates the conservation efforts of a nation. Although the common man considers the Wild Life (Protection) Act, 1972 (WLPA) as the only law that governs conservation in India, in fact there is a plethora of intertwined laws which the conservation agencies and the public have to wade through in their efforts to decide what actions to take or avoid. Apart from the

WLPA, there is the Indian Forest Act, 1927 (IFA); the Forest (Conservation) Act, 1980 (FCA); the Biodiversity Preservation Act, 2002 (BPA); The Scheduled Tribes and Other Traditional Forest Dwellers (Recognition of Forest Rights) Act, 2006 (FRA); and many state laws which have some similar and some contradictory provisions. For example, there is no basic difference between a reserve forest created under the IFA and a national park created under the WLPA but, inexplicably, we treat them differently. As forests (trees) and wildlife (animals) are a single integrated resource, they should have been dealt with under a single law. The mother of all forest laws, the IFA, could have been adapted to suit the emerging needs.

The multiplicity of laws creates difficulties both for the enforcement agencies as well as for the public. Even within the WLPA, which was specially crafted to deal with the needs of preserving our wild animals, there are so many unnecessary sections which either repeat what other sections say or contradict them, both causing difficulties in its implementation. For example, wild animals can be killed, surprisingly, inside national parks and sanctuaries for the sake of better management but not outside. This law came into existence primarily as a regulatory instrument for wildlife management, trade and utilisation, but over time, as a result of several amendments, it has become a completely prohibitory tool. In its current form, it has less to do with controlling the behaviour of the public vis a vis wildlife and is more of a tool to limit the states' control over their wildlife. A detailed examination of the legal framework is critical for the success of conservation but is beyond the scope of this book.

Apart from arguing that conservation should be based on modern thinking, local realities and the welfare of the rural communities, the book highlights the lopsided distribution of powers and responsibilities between the central and state governments, which makes conservation really difficult. This issue starkly stands out in the chapter "Tourism: A Conservation Tool." There seems to be a strong case for the empowerment of the states to make conservation decisions and also for keeping the central agencies out of operational decision making. I believe that any mistakes by the states can have only a local impact, but the same mistake by the entire country can have catastrophic implications.

This book would have been impossible if there had been no internet Most of the material quoted in the book has been accessed from the internet and has been used in the belief that it is correct. However, if a reader finds some content contrary to his own knowledge or belief, the author shall be grateful for such pointers.

I must admit that my thinking on conservation has been shaped primarily by my experiences in Madhya Pradesh. Although this analysis should be valid in most situations outside MP, in some cases the application may be a bit hazy. Readers are requested to keep this limitation in mind while pondering over the issues raised in this book.

I am aware of the fact that my views are in contradiction to the general approach to conservation in India and the book is likely to be controversial. I have gone over these thoughts millions of times with a view to find holes and chinks but could find none. Now it is all in the open and only the readers will decide whether these thoughts are the product of a crazed mind or a hint of fresh air that can infuse new life into conservation of wildlife in India.

Although most of my friends will not be surprised to see the contents of this book, strangers may be outraged at some apparently heretic statements coming from a person who was expected to believe otherwise. I am sure the apparent contradictions, between what I am saying and what I have been doing all my life, will disappear if they delve deeper into this short presentation. I have rarely met a person so far who does not accept the underlying truth of what I have said here, although I have seen people shocked when I begin saying these things.

So, welcome aboard!

2

Cultural Foundations of Conservation

The centrepiece of our current wildlife conservation paradigm is that wildlife is to be preserved only for moral, religious and ecological reasons and consumption of wildlife in any form is considered immoral and is prohibited by law.

The Wild Life (Protection) Act, 1972, which regulates the actions that affect the future of wildlife in India, does not allow the consumption of any wild animal and allows killing or capture of wild animals only in defence of human life and property (section 11) or for education and research (section 12). Animals in schedule I, which are more endangered than other species, can be killed only if they become a danger to human life (e.g., man-eating tigers) while others can be killed even if they are a threat merely to standing crops or other properties. The sentiment against the killing of animals is so strong that animals cannot be killed even for the sake of scientific management and can only be translocated to other habitats in cases of local overpopulation. All wild animals, dead or alive, procured legally or illegally, are government property (section 39) and only a very limited scope for possessing and transfer of wildlife goods exists. The Act had provisions for hunting and trade of wild animals and animal products at the time of its inception in 1972, but these were deleted over the years, although some vestiges of the original provisions still remain (e.g. section 44 – Dealings in trophy and animal articles without licence prohibited).

Contrary to the Indian practice, consumptive and non-consumptive benefits of wildlife drive the conservation programmes in many other countries. Although the current prohibition on hunting and trade in wildlife is primarily meant to guard against the overexploitation of already declining wild populations, it is generally believed that our religions and culture also proscribe hunting and consumption of wildlife. As no government enterprise can be sustained if it is in contradiction with the cultural beliefs of the people, it is necessary to examine the question as to whether our current conservation policy is in conformity with our cultural traditions.

Indian Culture and Wildlife

Although it is difficult to define the word "culture" precisely, it probably refers to a combination of traditions, lifestyles and vision of the people as shaped by the religious beliefs and past experiences of a society. The synonyms used for this word, in various dictionaries, are: civilisation, customs, traditions, mores, society, way of life, background, ethnicity, etc. More often than not, perhaps erroneously, culture is seen as coterminous with religion. Although modern Indian society is an amalgam of Hindu (and allied), Muslim, Christian and indigenous tribal cultural streams, we often allude to the Hindu part of our culture when we talk of Indian culture. Although vegetarianism is generally believed to be the core of the Indian or Hindu culture, neither the modern society is nor our Hindu ancestors have ever been completely vegetarian. As livestock was primarily kept for milk and draught purposes, most of the meat must have come from wild animals. There are numerous instances in our epics and religious scriptures which refute the belief that vegetarianism is a more pious way of life for human beings. We will look at some such examples later in this chapter.

We can easily imagine that before the dawn of civilisation the relationship between human beings and other animals must have been very simple, i.e. kill and eat whatever you can and hide from superior predators. With the emergence of assured food supplies as a result of domestication of animals and cultivation of plants, human dependence on hunting for food went down significantly, but we continued to kill wild animals for supplemental food supplies as well as to reduce the damages and threats caused by them. Apart from killing wild animals for necessity, hunting also became a means of recreation for the ruling classes over time. The interest in hunting as a means of recreation spread to the common man with the emergence of more egalitarian and democratic societies in recent times. The basic nature of our relationship with wild animals today is the same all over the world, with only minor variations.

Despite this fundamental truth, most of us believe that hunting and consumption of wildlife is contrary to Indian cultural traditions. However, a closer look at the Indian culture, history and religious texts leads one to the conclusion that Indian culture is no different from other cultures of the world as far as the sustainable utilisation of natural resources is concerned.

Conservation? No Word in Indian Languages

When I was appointed the Assistant Conservator of Forests, I knew what my job was: conservation. Not only did conservation sound like preservation, but it was actually believed to be the same thing. However, we were later told, during training, that, in fact, the word "conservation" is derived from two words, namely, "**con**sumption" and "pre**servation**". I tried to find out the source of this belief, for the purpose of this book, but found nothing on the internet to support this notion. In fact, this word is now applied to many disciplines and may have slightly different meanings in different fields.

For example, https://en.wiktionary.org/wiki/ conservation gives the following definitions of conservation:

- The act of preserving, guarding, or protecting; the keeping (of a thing) in a safe or entire state; preservation
- *Wise use of natural resources.*

- (<u>biology</u>) The discipline concerned with protection of <u>biodiversity</u>, the <u>environment</u>, and <u>natural resources</u>
- (<u>biology</u>) Genes and associated characteristics of biological organisms that are unchanged by evolution, for example similar or identical nucleic acid sequences or proteins in different species descended from a common ancestor
- (culture) The protection and care of cultural heritage, including artwork and architecture, as well as historical and archaeological artefacts
- (<u>physics</u>) lack of change in a measurable property of an isolated physical system (conservation of energy, mass, momentum, electric charge, subatomic particles, and fundamental symmetries)

In the case of natural resources, "the wise use of natural resources" seems to be quite apt and indicates that the perception that the word may actually have been derived from these two components (consumption and preservation) may actually be true. But none of the online dictionaries confirmed it.

The World Conservation Strategy (IUCN 1980) defines conservation as "The management of human use of the biosphere so that it may yield the greatest sustainable benefit to present generations while maintaining its potential to meet the needs and aspirations of future generations. Thus, conservation is positive, embracing preservation, maintenance, sustainable utilisation, restoration, and enhancement of natural environment." Conservation of natural resources clearly implies "sustainable utilisation" so that the resources are able to regenerate at least at the same rate at which they are consumed. Although the words "conservation" and "preservation" are generally treated as synonyms, "conservation" has a much broader connotation in the context of renewable natural resources. It seems the word "conservation" does not have an equivalent word in the Indian languages, particularly in Hindi. The Hindi words suraksha or sanrakshan, which are commonly used in translation, literally mean safety or protection, which is only a part — not the whole — of the concept of conservation. These Hindi expressions connote preservation alone, while conservation connotes preservation along with consumption. While conservation can literally be taken to mean "preservation along with consumption", signifying wise use or sustainable utilisation, preservation literally means "keeping something in existence or to keep safe from injury or harm". It had no connotation related to use or utilisation. Perhaps a new Hindi word, say "upakshan" [upyog (utilisation) + sanrakshan (preservation)] or upaksha [upyog (utilisation) + suraksha (protection or safety)] or suropyog (or suupyog) (wise use) [suraksha (safety) + upyog (utilisation)] should be coined to convey the complete meaning of the word "conservation" to the Indian minds. Perhaps surupyog (wise use) conveys the sense more clearly than the others.

Although the basic tenets of wise use (conservation) are the foundation of all cultures, as otherwise the culture itself would have been impossible, this difficulty in communicating the principle has resulted in a tremendous, and deadly, distortion of the concept of conservation in India. While the concept of consumption or utilisation is built into the philosophy of conservation, we seem to believe that conservation is possible only if there is no use, especially in the case of wildlife. This misunderstanding has taken such strong roots in our society that we almost instinctively have started believing that the only way to preserve wildlife is not to use it. However, man would like to preserve only those things which are of some use to mankind. If we cannot use wildlife, why preserve it? Why preserve something that is a dangerous pest? In fact, India was no exception to this culture of conservation. "Before the spread of extensive settled cultivation the Indian subcontinent would have been inhabited by territorial hunter-gatherers .... with cultural traditions of prudent resource use." (Madhav Gadgil and Romila Thapar).

Aldo Leopold, the undisputed father of modern wildlife management, quotes scriptures and historical records in illustrating how human cultures evolved by imbibing principles of conservation with sustainable utilisation as follows:

> ➤ "The tribes observing taboos which were biologically effective in preserving the game supply were more likely to survive and prosper .... than the tribes which did not." (<u>The History of Ideas</u>, page 5)

➢   The first written restrictions on the taking of game is probably that contained in the Mosaic Law. In the Book of the Covenant, ... Moses decrees:

"If a bird's nest chance to be before thee in the way, in any tree or on the ground, with young ones or eggs, and the dam sitting upon the young, or upon the eggs, thou shalt not take the dams with the young: thou shalt in any wise let the dam go, but the young thou mayest take unto thyself; that it may be well with thee, and that thou mayest prolong thy days." (Deuteronomy 22:6). (The History of Ideas, page 5)

➢   "---the first clear records of a well-rounded system of game management for conservation purposes is found not in Europe, but in the Mongol Empire. Marco Polo, in the narrative of his travels across Asia, thus describes the game laws of Kublai, "The Great Khan" (AD 1259-1294):

"There is an order which prohibits every person throughout all the countries subject to the Great Khan, from daring to kill hares, roebucks, fallow deer, stags, or other animals of that kind, or any large birds,, between the months of March and October. This is that they may increase and multiply; and as the breach of this order is attended with punishment, game of every description increases prodigiously." (The History of Ideas, page 6).

As there is a ban on the utilisation of wildlife for any purpose whatsoever, we in India seem to be preserving wildlife only for ecological, religious or moral reasons. We seem to be comfortable in the belief that the so-called Indian ethos, the *respect for all life,* will save our wildlife, despite the obvious fact that we are killing — of course illegally — more animals for eating or trading than are born. Most of this killing is done, not for becoming rich but for bare survival and sustenance, by the people who live with these animals and suffer their depredations. If that is true, perhaps our culture is not what it is purported to be. What we actually do is our culture, not what we believe it ought to be.

No Life without Consuming Other Lives

"*Jivo jivasya jeevanam,*" the verse from Srimad Bhagwat, is the ultimate truth of life. It unequivocally pronounces that "every organism is the food (life) of another". Those who swear by our scriptures need to look nowhere else in search of ecological wisdom. What the scripture says is that there can be no life without consuming other lives. To consume another organism, it has to be killed. Therefore, there is no way one can avoid killing as long as one lives. In the context of this truth, what we eat is more a question of convenience, availability and affordability, rather than a moral one.

It is interesting to examine the much exalted Indian ethos, the *respect for all life,* in relation to this fundamental truth. This concept probably emanates from the belief that God is present in all things, living and non-living. This belief is not unique to Indian or Hindu culture but is the basic tenet of most religions of the world. Those who believe that respect for all life means a complete abhorrence of killing or utilisation of other lives are obviously ignorant of the fact that such an interpretation of this philosophy, if accepted, will result in the end of life itself. In fact, life could not have begun on this earth in the first place if the primeval life forms had had to live by our philosophy. There can be no life without taking other lives, as food is nothing but bodies of other organisms. Life on this planet is sustained by the solar energy trapped by plants. Animals, including humans, can survive either by consuming the plants or other animals through which the energy travels in the food chains. Even plants cannot exist unless the existing plants die and release the nutrients consumed by them earlier for building the bodies of new generations of plants. A reasonable interpretation of the concept of *"respect for all life"* would, naturally, be that because diversity of life forms is important for sustaining the web of life on this earth, of which all species are a part, human beings must ensure that no extinctions result from their deeds. It cannot forbid the utilisation of other life forms for survival or progress. Our ancestors cannot have been so naive as to proscribe the use of the very fountainhead of life on this earth.

Although both plants and animals are living beings, we Indians — and several other civilisations — have historically believed that even inanimate things have life, consciousness, spirit, intelligence and even powers to influence other lives. Perhaps that is why we worship stones, books, pictures, statues, planets, stars, rivers, fire, lightening etc. But, strangely, we also believe that life in animals is somehow superior to the life in plants. Many of us think eating plants is fair game but eating animals is a sin. This partiality towards animals may be because, being animals ourselves, we understand and feel the pain, the cries, the bloodletting, etc. that accompany the killing of an animal much more intimately than the silent suffering and dying of a plant. This belief is not peculiar to Indian culture; it is a part of the universal human consciousness. But despite this feeling of our closeness to animals, consumption of wild animals and their products have sustained human survival and evolution till today. Thus meat eating is as natural to human beings, including Indians, as eating cereals, fruits and vegetables.

According to the *Household Consumption of Various Goods and Services* in India, 2011-12, released by the National Sample Survey Office (NSSO) in 2014, the percentage of Indians reporting consumption of eggs or meats during the previous 7 days is as follows:

Table 1: Consumption of Animal Foods in India

Food Item	% of Consuming Households in Previous 7 days.	
	Rural	Urban
Eggs	29.2	37.6
Fish/Prawn	26.5	21.0
Goat Meat	4.0	5.0
Chicken	21.7	27.0

Obviously, those who cannot afford to eat meat every week or eat other meats, including wild meat, are not recorded in the survey. The combined weight of these figures will easily be more than 50% of our population.

According to Arvind Kala (2005), although more vegetarians live in India than in the rest of the world, Indians are fast turning non-vegetarians. Degrees of vegetarianism vary from person to person. Indian vegetarians are mostly lacto-vegetarians who consume only milk products as an animal product. Some people eat fish and eggs and still call themselves vegetarians. Even though there are perhaps not many in India, there are extreme vegetarians, the vegans or fruitarians, who consider even dairy products an anathema. Perhaps the reluctance to eat meat stems from the reluctance to kill animals, as killing involves pain and bloodiness. Although Buddhism proscribes killing, most Buddhists do not mind eating meat of animals killed by others.

Although vegetarianism may have its health benefits, its universal practice will lead to the extinction of all or most of the domestic animals. There would have been no poultry, pigs, goats and sheep if humans were not eating them.

No doubt eating meat is a less energy efficient way of consuming resources, but this disadvantage is offset by the fact that through meat we can consume several materials, both of plant and animal origin, that we cannot consume directly but the food animals can. If human beings had to survive only on cultivated cereals and fruits, we would not have been able to support even a fraction of the current population. It is only because our livestock can feed on wild plants, which are inedible to humans, that we are more than six billion in number now. When we eat butter or meat, we are actually feeding on the grasses and forbs which make the bodies of our cattle and goats.

Obviously, meat eating is neither less moral than eating vegetarian food nor is it a wanton waste. Although some meat is also produced by feeding livestock on human grade cereals, especially in Western countries, we would need vastly more quantities of cereals and vegetables if everybody were to be a vegetarian. The tribals living in remote areas, whose food includes a significant proportion of wild meat, would find it difficult to survive only on grain produced on their marginal lands. Paradoxically, they also do a service to their better-off brethren by controlling the populations of wild ungulates, especially when there is a ban on legal hunting. If we do not control the populations of wild animals, they will run over our cities and villages. Populations of species like white-tailed deer in several states in the USA are exploding, which results in as many as 729,000 auto accidents per annum because there are not enough hunters to control them. If there was no hunting, the accidents in USA would grow at the rate of 218% per annum, costing them billions of dollars in auto repairs alone (IAFWA 2004).

Thus, it is obvious that meat eating is not only in conformity with the scheme of things which God seems to have had in mind while creating this world but also it is critical for human beings for social, economic and ecological reasons. Although we may have wiped out many species at the altar of our meat hunger, human existence would have been really precarious if we had had no meat eaters among us.

Meat Eating and Hunting in Scriptures and Epics

Although people try to justify our vegetarianism and ban on hunting wild animals on the basis of our religious scriptures, Indian mythology and history are replete with anecdotes of our most revered mythological and historical personalities hunting wild animals and eating them. Bharatratna Dr. PV Kane, believed to be one of the most respected Sanskrit scholars of India, discusses the religious diktats regarding meat eating in various scriptures in his eight volume treatise called the History of Dharamshastra. Although there are numerous references in our scriptures that indicate that meat eating was looked down upon by the creators of these scriptures, there is an equal number of references that indicate that meat eating has always been common and acceptable in India. However, Dr. Kane concludes that, "This is indeed surprising that meat eating is not considered good today while our ancestors and sages, etc. were non-vegetarians." Some of the important references mentioned by Dr. Kane in his book are mentioned below:

❖   The Rig Veda gives several indications that meat of bullocks was cooked. For example, the god

Indra says, "They cook 15-20 bullocks for me." (Rig Veda, verses 10.86.14 and 10.27.2).

❖ Offering meat to a guest entitles one to the rewards equivalent to that of a dwadshah yagya (Apastambdharamsutra verse 2.3.7.4).

❖ Yagyavalkya (1.258.260) writes that the (dead) ancestors remain satiated for several days, if the Brahmins are served a variety of meats at the shradh.

❖ There are long lists of birds that should be or should not be eaten in several writings, but jungle fowl and partridge are not prohibited.

❖ Chapter 5 of Manu Smriti deals extensively with meat eating issues in its 7th to 56th verses. Although several verses seem to contradict each other as to whether meat eating is good or not, it emerges unequivocally that meat eating was commonplace in vedic times. However, some of the verses that advocate meat eating are as follows:

➢ Brahmins can kill animals and birds, mentioned in the *shastras*, for feeding the *yagyas*, women, servants, etc. as Agastya (a revered sage) did the same (22).

➢ Edible deer and birds were first served at the *yagyas* performed by the rishis (sages), and then in those performed by the Brahmins and Kshatriyas (23).

➢ Even if one eats animals daily he is not debased as predators as well as prey have been created by Brahma only (30).

➢   Brahma has created plants and animals as food items only (28).

➢   Meat can be eaten if sanctified by the recitation of mantras, desired by the Brahmins, is as per the *shastras* permitted by the gurus and at difficult times (27).

➢   Eating meat, drinking liquor and sex are not sins as these are human nature (53)

➢   Along with meat, different kinds of dishes should be prepared at the time of shradh (feeding the dead) (verse 3.227).

❖   In Ramayana Retold by C. Rajgopalachari, several sections point out that Rama and family were hunters and ate meat regularly. For example:

➢   "Guha," said Rama, "I could indeed spend fourteen years in your kingdom as you desire. But would that be fulfilling my vow? I have left Ayodhya to fulfil my father's pledge. I must therefore lead the life of a *tapasvi*. I must not touch dishes daintily cooked and served. We have to live only on fruits, roots and permissible kinds of meat such as we offer in the sacrificial fire." (Chapter 19).

➢   Valmiki describes how Rama and Lakshmana secured food by hunting. He makes it quite plain that they had to subsist largely on meat (Chapter 20 – Chitrakoot).

➢   "I could take the aim by the ear and shoot, without seeing, a tiger or bear or other wild beast that might come to slake its thirst in the stream. I wanted to test this skill of mine. It was dense darkness. I waited for some wild animal to come. Then I heard a gurgling sound as of an elephant drinking. At once I aimed an arrow in the direction whence the sound came. Like a venomous serpent, swish went my dart and hit the object. But I was shocked to hear a human voice exclaim "Alas! I am dead!" I heard the man cry again piteously." (Chapter 22 – Idle Sport and Terrible Result).

➢ He (Jatayu, the vulture) said (to Rama): "When you leave Sita alone and go hunting in the forest, I shall be looking after her safety." (Chapter 31 – The Surpanakha Episode).

➢ "At once Maricha (a demon) transformed himself into a wonderful deer. ……. Lakshmana said, "This is no ordinary animal. This is a trick of the Rakshasas." But Sita said: "Do catch this deer for me. ……. If you cannot capture the creature alive, at least bring it down with an arrow and let us take the skin home. We shall never again see such a beautiful skin. It would be a lovely thing to sit on." (Chapter 35 – The Golden Stag)

❖ Rangarajan (2001) writes in India's Wildlife History that "When building their home in the forest, they (Rama, Laxman and Sita) first sacrificed that most essential of sacrificial animals, the blackbuck. Lakshmana made sure the animal was killed but left with its limbs intact to be cooked, broiled and only then offered to the gods."

❖ The following story from Mahabharata illustrates that sustainable hunting of wild animals was not forbidden during ancient times:

One night, Yudhishthira dreamt of seeing deer/antelope weeping and pleading with him at dawn. The king asked the trembling deer, who had folded hands, who they were and what they wanted to say and what they desired.

Thus, on being permitted by the Pandav King Yudhishthira, the honourable (yashsavi) son of Kunti, the surviving deer/antelope, said: "O Bharat! We are the deer of Dwait van (Dwait forest) who have escaped death. O King! Kindly do not give us any more pain. Please leave the Dwait Van and reside elsewhere. All you brothers are very brave (shurvir) and skilled in weapons. You have left very few wild animals alive. O Great Wise Man (mahamate)! The few of us left alive are just the seed (for rebuilding the population). O King Yudhishthir! With your kindness, we now want to grow.

On seeing those crazy (with grief), trembling deer, who were just enough to be the seed (for rebuilding the population), the king was pained and said: "Ok, this king wants the welfare of all beings. I will do as you desire."

Thus, on being wisened at the end of the night (dawn), the king Yudhishthira became kind to the deer and said to his brothers: "O Brothers! Tonight, the deer which have survived (our hunting) came to me and said: 'very few of us are left now, please have mercy on us.' They are telling the truth. We must have mercy on these wild animals. We have been using (hunting) them for nearly a year and six months (the brothers said).

There is a beautiful forest, called the Kamyak Van (Kamyak Forest), teeming with deer, which is situated at the head of the desert (maru bhumi), where there is a water tank (pond) called Trinabindu. We will set up our residence there and will enjoy ourselves."

Thereafter the Pandavas, who were well versed in all religions, left that forest along with all the brahmins and servants who were residing with them in the forest.

❖ According to Rangarajan (2001), "Long before the times referred to by the Sanskrit texts, wild animals were a major source of meats in the various sites of the Harappan civilization."

❖ The ancient treatise Arthshastra reveals that the Mauryas designated specific forests to protect supplies of timber, as well as lions and tigers for skins. Elsewhere, the Protector of Forests also worked to eliminate thieves, tigers and other predators to render the woods safe for grazing cattle.

❖ The rock edicts erected by King Asoka (269 BC to 231 BC) of the same dynasty give us a glimpse of the relationship of the people with wildlife at the time. The Major Rock Edict at Girnar proclaims that "....... no living beings are to be slaughtered or offered in sacrifice —," after the king embraced Buddhism. The same rock edict informs us that, "Formerly, in the kitchen of ....

King Priyadasi (Asoka), hundreds of thousands of animals were killed every day .... but now .... only three creatures, two peacocks and a deer are killed, and the deer not always." (Dhammika, 1993). This seems to be an exaggeration but shows that eating wild animals has been a part of our culture. The edicts show that "Asoka did not completely prohibit the killing of animals; he prohibited gratuitous killings (such as sacrifice); he advocated restraint in the number that had to be killed for consumption; protected some of them .... The legal restrictions conflicted with the practices then freely exercised by the common people in hunting, felling, fishing and setting fires in forests." (Wikipedia).

Conclusion

These references from the holy, as well as the worldly, books illustrate that hunting of wild animals for food has always been a part of the Indian culture, like all other great cultures of the world. Inclusion of *"jivo jivasya jeevanam"*, i.e. one organism is the food for another, in Srimad Bhagwat Purana, which is one of the most popular *puranas*, clearly clinches the issue that neither our religion prohibits using other animals as human food nor has such a culture ever been practiced in history. Food preferences of different sections or castes may have varied based on the prevailing beliefs or socioeconomic compulsions, but it seems to have had nothing to do with religious edicts. If the prevailing ban on hunting was indeed in reverence to a particular interpretation of our culture, such thinking would have been reflected in our laws and other instruments of governance all along. It is difficult to believe that we suddenly woke up to our cultural mores in 1991, as the Wild Life (Preservation) Act, 1972, had a complete set of provisions, as mentioned before, to allow and regulate hunting of wild animals until then.

Therefore, the Indian religions, ethos, culture, traditions — whatever we call it — do not seem to support our current conservation policies. As such, the only justification for them is our fear that if we allow hunting of wild animals, we may be unable to regulate the removal to keep it within sustainable limits. This is a reasonable and logical consideration and would have been an impeccable foundation for our conservation framework if it had worked. The tragedy, however, is that wildlife is being exploited — entirely illegally — far beyond its rates of reproduction, despite the ban on hunting. This is primarily because, contrary to popular belief, hunting is a cultural and socioeconomic requirement to a large part of our society and cannot be eliminated merely through a legal ban or prohibition. Whether we admit or not, wildlife is a commodity of mass consumption and people will seek it out and use it if available. Several studies have confirmed that bitter truth. For example:

❖ Madhusudan & Karanth (2002) found that 216 man days of hunting takes place in every village around the Nagarhole and Kundremukh national parks of Karnataka.

❖   Ambika Aiyadurai of the Nature Conservation Foundation (NCF) showed that nearly everybody in Arunachal Pradesh hunts — some full time, some part time — and that nearly everyone owns a gun. During the survey, 27 mammals, 18 birds and 2 reptiles were seen served as meat. Wild meat is served at every important function and is sold from INR 50 (dried) to INR 100 (fresh) a kilo.

❖   In a similar study, Hilaluddin, *et al.* (2005) found that villagers had hunted 134 species of wild animals and birds in the previous year, and households consumed 278 kg to 545 kg of wild meat annually. Also, 773 dead animals of 53 species were actually seen by the researchers in 15 days of observation in the Kohima markets alone.

❖   Chutia and Solanki (2013) found that 53 species of birds, including 18 from schedule I of the WPA, are hunted by tribals in Arunachal Pradesh.

❖   Verrier Elwin (1939), who worked with tribal communities in many states in the early part of the twentieth century, was informed by a Baiga tribal of Central India in the following words: "*But our minds are never satisfied without meat. Even if Government make a hundred laws that we are not to hunt, we will do it. One of us will keep the official talking, and the rest will go off to the jungle and get a good, fat deer.*" Another Baiga says that, "*Secretly, we kill sambhar, hiran (blackbuck), gutri (barking deer), hares, lil (blue bull), chital, mangwari (mouse deer), mongoose, peacock, and bring them home and eat them with great delight."* Elwin further says that Baigas are said to distinguish 21 different kinds of rats and they eat them all. Describing the hunting culture of the Baiga tribe, Elwin describes nearly a dozen kinds of traps used by the Baigas to trap animals and birds. He quotes one Colonel Ward as saying that Baigas are *"first-rate sportsmen .... very expert in all the appliances of the chase — good shots with their small bows and arrows."*

❖ Elvin also quotes Forsyth (1871), saying that Baigas "eke out the fruits of the earth by an unwearing pursuit of game. Full of courage and accustomed to depend on each other, they hesitate not to attack every animal of the forest, including the tiger."

The same is likely to be true of most other forest-dwelling tribes. While arguing that the Baigas should be allowed to hunt wildlife in conformity with their cultural traditions, Elvin mentions the hunting traditions of several Indian tribes. He says, "The Baiga still .... enjoys the freedom of the forest, but he does so with a guilty mind. It seems to me essential that this feeling of guilt should be removed. The Game Act has pressed heavily upon the Baiga and has served still further to devitalize tribal life. .... It would be a very good thing if the Baiga were at least allowed an annual hunt. .... The *Bhatra* used to have a ceremonial hunt in March preliminary to the *Bijphutni* festival in honour of Mati Deo, god of hunting. The *Gadba* do the same even now and cook the game in the presence of Mati Deo; if they fail, their women pelt them with cow-dung. It is during the tribal hunt that the Santal come together as a tribe and settle their major problems. One of the chief Rajput festivals was the Aheria, the spring hunting. So is the *Sekrengi* of the *Angami* Naga, the *Jur Sital* of Bihar, the hunting festival of the Halrakki Vakkal of Kanara. If the Baiga were allowed one great hunt, this would have a revivifying effect on tribal life and might even benefit the game in the long run for they would be less likely to poach at other times. The killing of hares should, in any case, be permitted and it should not be illegal to carry bows and arrows."

What was true a hundred years ago is equally true today. I have personally seen small tribal children in Bastar, in Chhattisgarh, bring down a bird, sitting nearly 50 m away, with their crude sling shots.

Apart from the resident agrarian or hunting gathering communities, there are several nomadic hunting communities, such as the *pardhis, bawarias, bahelias, chirimars, saperas, naths, mogias,* etc., which traditionally lived only on the hunting and trapping of wild animals, for self-consumption as well as for cash. They virtually continue to live the same way, although some of them have tried to adopt new vocations such as selling cheap cosmetics, dealing in domestic scrap, selling fake medicines, and even begging, along with sundry crimes. As their combined numbers are significant, and most of them still live fully or partly off wildlife, their impact on wildlife is huge. The rich and feudal families hunt wildlife for fun and recreation and often take serious risk by breaking the law in pursuit of their penchant to hunt. Of course there are international wildlife smugglers, Sansar Chands and their ilk, who use these hunting communities to procure supplies of skins, bones, ivory and several other items for their syndicates, and further fuel the poaching of wild animals. It needs no genius to understand that it will be a herculean task to control it only with the help of the law. Even Asoka the Great knew that enforcement of a universal ban on hunting of wildlife was impossible (Rangarajan 2001).

The dominant position of the Homo *sapiens* among all species is a testimony that this species has been able to utilise the earth's resources better than other species. Therefore, our culture consists of those resource-use practices and traditions which have enabled us to survive on this planet since the appearance of our species on this earth.

From the foregoing discussion, it is reasonable to conclude that our prevailing conservation philosophy has nothing to do with our culture and ethos. Perhaps bringing it in consonance with our culture can make conservation much more acceptable to the common man, and viable in the long term.

3

Our Blurred Vision

All enterprises are created for achieving certain predefined goals. And all good enterprises try to set measurable and achievable goals. These goals may have to be modified in the light of past performance and changing circumstances. Accordingly, our National Forest Policy of 1988 says that the country will endeavour to have 33% of its total geographic area under forests. To further focus on critical ecosystems and endangered species, the National Biogeographic Report (Rodgers et al. 2002), indicates that we need to put approximately 5-10% of each biome under protected status (national parks and wildlife sanctuaries) in order to create a network of protected areas representing all our natural ecosystems and the habitats of endangered species. Although the National Biogeographic Report (2002-2016) is not an official policy statement of the government, the targets mentioned in this document are generally treated as the national conservation goals. Similarly, our National Wildlife Action Plan ordains that we need to put 10% of the Indian landmass under protected area status, of which at least half should be inviolate habitats. This will be close to half of our forest area. These targets represent our minimum wish list; if we can have more forests or more coverage under protected areas, it will be even better.

All the forest areas produce timber and wild animals, as well as several other products, and the capacity of a habitat to produce goods depends, to a significant extent, on its management. All over the world, timber production areas are managed on the principle of "maximum sustained yield" in perpetuity. It would have been logical for us to have a similar management goal for producing wild animals as well. But none of the national policy, legal or management documents makes any statement indicating the ultimate aim or goal of our wildlife preservation programmes. This may be because we never thought of using them as an economic resource and their ecological role is not critical, because the functions they perform can easily be performed by human beings. We have always justified the preservation of wildlife because that will also preserve wild lands, which conserve our soil, water and other biodiversity and also produce healthy air. Accordingly, all the policy instruments aim to provide maximum protection to wildlife, which means we do want to produce a maximum number of wild animals from a given area.

As there is no concept of "yield" or harvest of wild animals in India, we have not bothered to define the goals of wildlife management clearly. Another reason for not setting clear-cut goals for producing wildlife is, perhaps, our sub-conscious belief that we are never going to be really successful in conservation. And we are correct. If wild animals cause only harm and suffering to people, and if people can benefit by killing animals, though illegally, they will continue to kill more animals than we will ever produce through our conservation programmes.

But suppose the unthinkable happens and we are successful in producing lots and lots of animals of all species. We will then have to decide what animals to produce in preference to others, depending on relative costs (no benefits, mind it). The cost of producing wildlife comes primarily in two forms. One is the cost of protecting and managing wildlife and its habitat, paid by the government from the exchequer. The other cost pertains to the losses incurred by the forest dwelling people in the form of opportunity cost of losing access to their neighbourhood forests, crop losses and livestock deaths.

Contrasting Stakes

Our society can be roughly divided into three segments on the basis of their possible stakes in the preservation of wildlife.

- One segment, consisting of the people primarily living in urban and semi urban areas far away from wildlife habitats, wants wildlife to be preserved because they think, if for nothing else, it is morally right to have wildlife in the country. This section is the very large majority of our population, living in 80% of our landmass. This section does not suffer any adverse effects of having wild animals because they live far away from them.

- The second segment comprises the professionals and businessmen, and their employees, who actually profit from wild animals, as their jobs and businesses depend upon them. They include conservation NGOs, foresters, authors, filmmakers and people in the tourism industry.
- The third section is the silent minority living in 20% of our landmass that supports forests and other natural ecosystems. They would be better off if there were no wild animals to contend with on a daily basis.

The decision to have wildlife is made by the unaffected majority, but whether these decisions will bear results depends upon the will of the people who have to live with, and suffer, these animals.

Vision for the Future

We, the unaffected or profiting people, have given to the country the following vision regarding wild animals:

- We want self-sustaining populations of all big mammals in all government forests.
- We expect our forest dwelling siblings to bear the losses caused by wild animals stoically.
- We want no benefits from wild animals for the society, not even for those who suffer their depredations.

This is the sum of our collective beliefs. Although these elements of our national conservation endeavour are not codified anywhere, we all believe in them subconsciously. We have been implementing this policy since 1972 and the result, with several local ups and downs, shows that the numbers and spread of most species have shrunk drastically. Although the current tiger population (2226) is reported to be significantly higher now than 1827 estimated in 1972 this may not really be true as the methodologies used in both assessments were quite different.

Let us examine these tenets in some detail.

Self-Sustaining Populations in All Forests

Our forests were always meant for wild animals although these were not specially manipulated to produce more animals, except in protected areas. Although different species of animals may have different habitat requirements, such as dense woodland, open woodland, grassland, etc., we do not do any fine forest management for creating such habitat blocks even in PAs. We consider a blanket ban on exploitation of forests adequate for all purposes, as most natural forests do provide such habitat diversity to different degrees. The only forest or habitat management we do in PAs is the provision of adequate drinking water and improvement of grasslands. Such management is considered best for increasing tigers and their prey base. Silvicultural operations such as afforestation, felling, thinning, pruning, etc. are not considered compatible with good wildlife management. Therefore, such practices are not followed in PAs.

WLPA now provides, since 2006, that the tiger conservation plans of tiger reserves have to ensure that "the forestry operations of regular forest divisions .... are not incompatible with the needs of tiger conservation" [section 38V (2) (c)]. This is "to provide dispersal habitats and corridor for spill over population of wild animals from designated core areas of tiger reserves or from tiger breeding habitats within other protected areas" [section 38V (2) (b)]. As wild animals have always been present in our forests, even under traditional forest management, this new provision only intends to enhance their densities outside PAs. This obviously means that all forests in tiger-bearing states now have to be managed like those in protected areas, particularly tiger reserves. That means there will be no exploitation for timber, bamboo or non-wood forest produce (NWFP) for human consumption even in forests outside PAs. We also need to prohibit the grazing of livestock in all forests, as livestock competes with tiger's prey base for resources. Obviously, such a forest management is impossible, particularly for a country like India where millions of people depend on these forests for their day to day needs. It will also be a serious loss of revenue for some states. For example, MP earned INR 871.25 crore from forest management in year 2011-12, which will be lost if this provision is complied with. So, nothing is likely to change on the ground, and the wildlife populations outside PAs are unlikely to improve, despite this provision.

The absurdity of the situation does not end here. Although the WLPA provides protection to wild animals against poaching everywhere, PAs were particularly created for their security and proliferation. With the advent of the Project Tiger in 1973 came the concept of buffer zones, surrounding the core zones (national parks or wildlife sanctuaries) administered by the tiger reserve authorities to provide extra security to animals spilling out of the core zones. Since 2006, the buffer zones have also acquired the sanctity of a protected area and are now protected under the WLPA also. All forests have now acquired the status of a wildlife corridor as nothing "ecologically unsustainable", i.e. not in the interest of wildlife, can be done in these forests without the consent of NTCA and the National Board for Wild Life (NBWL), as per section 38 O (g) of the WLPA. Not only this. As this section provides the same protection against "ecologically unsustainable" land use to PAs and other *lands*, the entire country is now virtually a PA.

While it is impossible to provide reasonable protection to wild animals outside PAs (the reason for creating PAs) everywhere in the country, as these landscapes have a strong human wildlife interface, empowering NTCA and NBWL to intervene in land use changes anywhere in the country has serious implications, both for conservation as well as for the economic development of the country. As a large number of development projects have been blocked or delayed due to these additional provisions — making the country pay dearly for strengthening conservation — GoI is already planning to dilute all environmental laws to ease the process of development. Obviously, this is a backlash to an overambitious conservation agenda, which our careless legislators approved not many years ago. Earlier, only the local people were troubled by wildlife, now even the distant people have to suffer due to delayed or blocked development projects. As the development lobbies are much stronger than the so-called greens, it is only a question of time before we see the backlash hitting us with full force. Soon we may even have to live with much more weakened wildlife laws than before.

But, even if this prescription that all forests are to be managed for tiger conservation is followed, the spill over animals from PAs are likely to continue to perish, as usual, in conflict with local communities or due to easier poaching opportunities. We have little wildlife left outside PAs, despite legal protection, and things are unlikely to change unless wild animals promise some benefit to the local people. As neither our law nor any policy documents direct the state to generate benefits for the society from wild animals, animals near villages are going to continue to be only a menace for the local people. Therefore, it is not possible to have self-sustaining wildlife populations everywhere unless the basic relationship between human beings and wild animals changes.

Not to speak of general forests, it is difficult to have self-sustaining populations of all species even in PAs. Most of our wildlife habitats support complex wildlife communities consisting of many species of predators and many species of prey. All species in a community are related to each other through competition or predation. Cases of symbiosis and commensalism, much romanticised by the TV channels, especially among marine species, are rather rare among large mammals. Predators like tigers, leopards and wild dogs compete among themselves for prey while the herbivores like chital, sambars, barasingha and wild pigs compete among themselves for food and other resources. Despite so-called niche separation between apparent competitors, these species still compete with each other for the total available biomass at appropriate trophic levels and thereby control each other's populations. For example, high tiger densities are believed to depress leopard densities in many parks. In the nineties, the managers of Satpura National Park used to explain the low tiger density being due to a high density of wild dogs. For over 20 years, the population of highly endangered hard-ground barasingha in Kanha did not improve because of a high predator population supported by an abundant chital population, as well as competition with chital for habitat. The situation improved only when tiger numbers reportedly went down from 105 in 2000 to approximately 60 in 2010.

Thus it is obvious that we are now living in an ocean of contradictions. While the law requires that we establish good wildlife populations everywhere in the forests, neither the forest departments can do that nor the people of this country want that to happen.

No Benefits to Society

Wildlife can generate economic benefits for people through tourism and hunting. One can understand the ban on hunting as a precautionary measure against overexploitation, but why we have decided to forego all benefits from wild animals is inexplicable. There has been no legal hunting of wildlife in the country, except perhaps some duck shooting, since the early seventies, although the law banned it only in 1991. Wildlife tourism, which is a natural product of modern conservation, barely escaped being banned by GoI-NTCA combine in 2012 and shall be practiced only in a very stymied form in future as a result of the extremely restrictive government guidelines and an atrocious interpretation of the law.

It is a fact that sustainable benefits can be secured for the society by removing the disposable animals from all wildlife populations. The whole world practices this credo. Whether we want benefits or not, some animals have to be removed from wildlife populations for their own sake as well. This may be necessary for keeping the habitat in a healthy condition, or to maintain optimal age and sex ratios, or to keep a balance between competing species. At present the poachers are doing that job for us. If there had been no poachers, the opposition of the local people to conservation would have been much more severe as the losses would have been much higher. If we have to do this job officially and burn or bury the carcasses of the animals that we may have to kill, as per the current practice, the cost of capturing or killing animals legally can be unimaginable. For example, the cost of culling surplus animals in the US has been estimated to be approximately $3100 per animal. On the contrary, the income to the society if the populations are regulated through sport hunting is estimated to be $3550 per animal, making the virtual income from hunting $6650 (3100+3550) per animal. It is further estimated that 37.4 million American hunters and anglers contributed approximately 89.8 billion dollars to the US economy in 2011 (USFWS and CB 2014), while the potential losses from road accidents, crop losses, losses to the timber industry, etc. could be as high as $70 billion per annum if there was no hunting (IAFWA 2005). The cost of culling half as many animals as the hunters take in a year in the US can be more than 9 billion dollars per annum (IAFWA 2005).

Poachers and the local people are saving us these costs of culling or translocation by keeping the wildlife populations low! And we have made poachers out of millions of forest dwelling humans by outlawing the utilisation of wildlife. As they will suffer if wildlife flourishes, people have to take steps to keep wildlife populations down by killing and eating them. In many countries, including the US, wild animals can be killed by farmers on their property. But in India a farmer can only shoo animals away from his crops. So, people kill them illegally. Thus, irrespective of whether we officially want to benefit from wildlife or not, someone is going to benefit as long as wildlife is around. If these benefits had been guaranteed through a legal system, local people would have been careful about what they take in order to ensure the sustainability of the benefits. Moreover, the benefits could have been enhanced many fold by proper marketing of the hunting opportunities to the rich, so that they pay, just for the pleasure of hunting, many times the value of the meat and trophies that would normally accrue to a poacher. As of now, it is a virtual free for all and an animal belongs to whoever takes it first. And if 120 million people — more than the entire populations of several countries — living inside our forested tracts have to kill wild animals, even occasionally, to survive, we should not be surprised at the dismal state of affairs. If we had been preserving wildlife for economic reasons, where more animals would have meant more legal benefits to the society — especially the forest-side communities — we would have had as many animals as our forests could possibly hold and support.

As discussed in the chapter on tourism, wildlife tourism is one of the most important conservation innovations of modern times. Wildlife tourism drives conservation all over the world as wild animals and wild spaces are specially preserved for the enjoyment of the public. The economic benefits generated by tourism force governments to put more and more areas under conservation and manage them better and better (Higginbottom *et al.* 2001). It is estimated that nearly 71.8 million Americans, 31% of the national population, spend nearly $54.9 billion as non-hunting wildlife tourists (USFWS and CB 2014). As every dollar spent by visitors results in the production of jobs and livelihoods, the kind of employment that such traffic can generate cannot be overestimated. India must be the only country in the world which wants to leave no scope for the growth of wildlife tourism in the future, despite having some of the finest wild vistas on earth.

The guidelines issued by NTCA (2012) for tourism in tiger reserves provide that the tourism zones cannot be enlarged. As more and more of the existing PAs are being converted into tiger reserves where wildlife tourism shall not be allowed to grow beyond the present negligible levels, conservation will have to find some other reason to sustain itself in India as the economic benefits of wildlife tourism as the justification for conservation of dangerous animals is now ruled out. We either have to change this approach or conservation will collapse under its own weight as the country will not be able to afford the direct and opportunity costs. Fortunately, tourism is one of the priority areas (5Ts -- talent, tradition, tourism, trade and technology) on which the new government in Delhi is planning to build its "Brand India". Whether the Ministry of Environment, Forests and Climate Change (MoEFCC) and NTCA are still able to keep wildlife tourism as an island of neglect will be interesting to see.

Perhaps, in the not so distant future, things will change. Along with the newfound emphasis of the government on using tourism as a driver of economic development, we are hearing that MoEFCC is also going to encourage the hunting of crop-raiding wildlife. Bihar recently hired a professional hunter to kill about a dozen blue bulls for crop raiding. Rather than just declaring them as vermin and allowing their indiscriminate destruction, as seems to be the thinking in MoEFCC at present, we can convert this situation into an economic opportunity by introducing sport hunting of the target populations to generate revenues, rather than spending money on their destruction.

Local People Will Continue to Bear the Cost of Conservation

As discussed before, there are two kinds of costs to conservation in poor countries. The government pays for the maintenance of the conservation agencies, like the forest departments and their operations. We all know this cost. But the cost borne by the local people for maintaining our wildlife is generally not taken into consideration by most analysts. This cost primarily includes the value of crops and livestock eaten by wild animals, crop protection costs, as well as the livelihood options foregone by the people if they happen to be living close to a protected area. Although many states have introduced compensation systems for the losses incurred by the people, these are mostly cosmetic in nature as little money reaches the people because of our poor delivery systems for public services. The primary reason for the failure of conservation in India, despite legal protection to wild animals everywhere, is that we continue to believe that the affected people will continue to bear the losses without reacting, despite overwhelming evidence to the contrary. As our forests are progressively getting emptied of wild animals, it is evident that the local people are reacting to keep their losses down.

Although people continue to live even inside our PAs, despite legal requirements to the contrary, our corridors or the managed forests connecting the PAs in particular are thickly punctuated with villages. In Madhya Pradesh, a state with a relatively better forest-to-man ratio, there are nearly 22,000 villages situated within a five km radius of 95,000 km^2 of its forest area, giving an average of one village in every 4.5 km^2 of forest, or at approximately 1.25 km distance from each other. While local people occupy all such small patches of forests, grazing their livestock, collecting fuel wood and other products, wild animals raid their crop fields for sustenance. This is a strong recipe for conflict between men and wildlife, in which animals always come second best. While people use traps, snares, poisons and live wires to kill animals, they themselves suffer tremendous crop losses and discomfort. People have to spend approximately 200 days and nights a year, mostly in the cold winter and pouring rains, protecting their crops against wild animals, living a perilous existence. Although no precise estimates of crop losses due to wildlife raids are available, a rapid assessment in 2002 indicated an average loss of INR 1070 ($18) per annum per hectare, leading to a total loss worth INR 94 crores ($15.6 mn) and labour investment in crop protection worth INR 526 ($87.6 mn) crores per annum in fields lying within two km of the forest boundary (Pabla 2005). These costs must be several times more if calculated at current prices.

Mishra (1997) found out that approximately half the annual average income of a family is lost to carnivore depredations on livestock in the Indian trans-Himalaya, while the government compensation amounted to only 3% of the perceived annual loss.

Madhusudan *et al.* (2003) estimated that villagers lost 12% of their livestock and 11% of their grain production to wildlife in the Bhadra Tiger Reserve between 1996 and1999, while the compensation received from the Government amounted to only 5% and 14% of the losses.

Maikhuri *et al.* (2001) studied the human-wildlife conflict around the Nandadevi Biosphere Reserve and found that more than 90% of respondents perceived that the rural economy had deteriorated due to crop damages, livestock lost to wildlife, termination of opportunities to harvest medicinal plants, and tourism in the core zone of the reserve. The mean economic loss was estimated at 1285 rupees ($21.41), 1195 rupees ($19.92), and 156 ($2.6) rupees from wildlife damage to food crops, fruit trees, and beehives, respectively.

These losses hurt even more as the affected people are mostly the poorest citizens of India. Whether wildlife will survive outside PAs under such dire circumstances is anybody's guess.

We must, however, admit that losses due to wildlife depredations are inevitable when people and wild animals live shoulder to shoulder. If people were free to protect themselves against wild animals by whatever means, lethal or non-lethal, as they had done in the past, we can say that the government has no obligation to help them. But because our law does not allow people to use lethal means to protect themselves, it is incumbent on the government to compensate the losses imposed by the government on the local people. The responsibility of the government is to help people in minimising these losses and compensating them for whatever losses occur despite taking mitigating measures. Perhaps no Indian state has any programme to prevent wildlife damage to crops, except some trenches and power fences in elephant-bearing states. Compensation programmes for losses of crops and livestock do exist in most states, but these systems hardly make any difference to the attitude of the people towards wildlife. This is because, on one hand, these programmes do not provide for compensating the losses completely, and on the other, the cumbersome procedures, corruption and ignorance reduce the efficacy of these programmes to negligible levels. For example, when Madhya Pradesh introduced the programme for compensating crop losses in 2008, we directed our field officers to publicise the scheme extensively. However, despite the publicity, the growth in the number of claims was not adequate in the next 2-3 years. We discovered, to our horror, that while only 3 cases had reached the DFO's office, more than 3000 applications for compensation had been received in various field offices in Chhatarpur district alone. On a recent visit to the Radhanagari wildlife sanctuary in Maharashtra, I found that despite having perhaps one of the best compensation rates in the country, claims for crop damage by gaur had not been decided for two years. With such poor delivery systems, it is difficult to imagine that compensation can ever be an effective tool in conservation.

Even if the compensation systems work satisfactorily, the scale and quantum of losses is so large that it is going to be impossible for any government to compensate the losses fully. Therefore, in the absence of effective systems of regulating the populations of problem species, especially the crop raiding ones, the forest dwelling communities are likely to continue to be the victims of our wildlife preservation programmes.

We, very nostalgically, talk that at the turn of the last century, India had nearly 40,000 wild tigers in the country, while we now have only about two thousand. If we want to revert to the same number of tigers, the number of other animals will also have to grow twenty times, at least. As a result, our losses to wild animals will also go up proportionately, to be borne by the poor forest dwelling communities. So, if we do not want to sacrifice our poor countrymen at the altar of conservation, we will have to stop tigers and other animals from growing beyond a limit, much before the fancied figure of 40,000. Karanth *et al.* (2004) believe that Indian forests can still sustain about 20,000 tigers, but this will be prohibitively expensive in terms of human suffering, unless these animals and their prey base could be put to some productive use to compensate the losses.

Our Conservation Paradigm

The paradigm we have created for realising our conservation goal is enshrined in the Wildlife (Protection) Act, 1972. It consists of the following two components:

- Constitution of protected areas (national parks, sanctuaries, tiger reserves) for wildlife;

- Complete ban on consumption, possession and trade in wild animals and products.

Both these pillars of conservation in India have shown limited results in securing our wildlife.

With some notable exceptions, the protected areas (PAs) have failed to show any significant increase in the populations of the endangered species for whom these PAs were created. Although we have been losing endangered species from our PAs for a long time, the recent loss of entire tiger populations from the Sariska and Panna tiger reserves has highlighted the limitations of this approach. Sixteen other tiger reserves are almost without tigers, as per the government's own admission (DNA 13 August, 2009: http://bigcatrescue.org/50-of-tiger-reserves-in-bad-shape/). As mentioned before, we lost black buck from Kanha (MP), great Indian bustard from Karera (MP), and gaur from Bandhavgarh (MP). The barasingha population in Kanha was stagnating around 300-400 animals for nearly three decades, although the population seems to be growing again as new habitats have become available due to the relocation of more villages since 2010. There may be several other unrecorded extinctions or depletions in protected areas which were meant to preserve these species. This clearly indicates that either the so-called protected areas are not really protected or that protection alone is not good enough to preserve our wildlife. Probably both these possible inferences are true. Effective protection is virtually impossible where animals can go out and poachers can come in through the open boundaries of the so-called protected areas. Although these protected areas are meant to be created by moving people out, people continue to live inside most PAs, at a tremendous cost both to humans and wild animals, despite nearly four decades of conservation.

The proscription of consumption and trade in wildlife is as ineffective as the prohibition of drinking imposed from time to time by various states. While every state, with the only exception of Gujarat, has abandoned its policy of prohibition, we are reluctant to review our policy of outlawing use of wildlife. There is no doubt that overhunting, which is of course illegal, has led us to the current state of affairs. As a result, we have developed an instinctive repugnance towards hunting, remaining benignly oblivious of the fact that several countries, especially in the developing world, with similar histories of the overhunting of their wildlife by the local people have reversed the decline by reintroducing regulated hunting by tourists, ensuring significant economic benefits and jobs to the local communities who would otherwise poach these animals. If local people associate economic benefits with abundance of wildlife, and if incomes from tourists and hunting can be demonstrated to be more than that by hunting themselves, they will not only stop poaching animals themselves but will also stop outside poachers from stealing their animals.

Humans and Wild Animals Need Each Other

Although man's relationship with wild animals has evolved with time, there is no denying the fact that they have been an integral part of each other's environment forever. In the beginning, men and wild animals must have been food for one another, until men realised the value of domesticating some species. Men have always tried to eliminate the dangerous animals and preserve the useful game species, until recently when we realised that even dangerous predators deserve our protection for various reasons. Even the game species came in conflict with men as they started raiding agriculture and were tolerated only to the extent they could be hunted for food. We human beings have wiped out several species from this earth because they were either considered dangerous and harmful or they were so useful that too many people hunted too many of them.

In contrast to the wild animals, our domestic animals are in no danger of extinction, just because they became economically useful to man. However, original races and varieties of domestic species are continuously being replaced by more productive and profitable ones — so much so that we have to mount special conservation programmes to preserve the gene pool of the replaced varieties. Our wildlife is in the same situation as the older races of the domestic animals and plants: they both are endangered just because they are not profitable enough for human beings. Perhaps nobody can stop this inexorable march into extinction unless we find ways of making wild animals a viable economic asset

Wildlife continues to thrive and has made impressive comebacks from the brink in some cases in those countries where its economic benefits, particularly to the local communities, outweigh the losses due to their depredations. Nearly all the game and predator species in Africa are in reasonably good condition, as they generate impressive returns for those countries from tourism, sport hunting or both. In Pakistan's NWFP, the critically endangered Suleiman markhor (Capra *falconeri megaceros)* and several associated species have returned from the brink due to the path-breaking, community-based, trophy hunting program that has replaced the free-for-all poaching since the early nineties (Edwards 2006). The fabled American bison, which almost disappeared from this earth by the late nineteenth century, is again attracting millions of tourists to the USA and Canada and is again being subjected to sustainable hunting, even culling.

Conclusion

It is obvious from the above discussion that our national goal of having wild animals in all forests, despite tremendous opportunity and direct costs to the local people without any legal benefits from animals, is not based on ground realities. Our vision about wildlife seems truncated and incomplete. Any enterprise that produces something knows what to do with the produce. We have set about producing wildlife in our forests as a national endeavour but have still not decided what to do with the animals we produce. This is extremely strange, especially for a poor country, because every animal we produce entails severe cost and human suffering. It seems we are producing wild animals just for dying a natural death, although most of them are actually being killed by the neighbouring communities. This incomplete vision has reduced wildlife management to be a passive production regime, blocking the development of efficient conservation techniques and technologies as well as investment of private capital in conservation. Although the conservation agencies think the resources allocated by the government for conservation are grossly inadequate, whatever public investments go into conservation seem to be a waste as they are not producing any results. Neither our habitats nor wildlife populations are improving. If conservation could attract private investments to complement public spending under a new policy paradigm, the chances of success can be increased exponentially. The country should, therefore, consider giving itself a new conservation goal.

A New Conservation Goal

In view of the foregoing, it will be pertinent to redefine our conservation goal both in terms of clarity of intent as well as to bring it in tune with the ground realities. The best way to define a conservation goal is to borrow the essence of its definition, as given in the World Conservation Strategy. A reasonable goal for conservation of wildlife shall then be:

The management of wildlife populations and habitats so that it may yield the greatest sustainable benefit to present generations, especially the local people, while maintaining its potential to generate sustainable benefits for future generations.

This goal does not require us to make impossible sacrifices to protect wild animals. If the current generations, especially the forest side communities, benefit from wildlife, they will try to ensure that the benefits are passed on to the future generations as well. If wild animals are a source of pain to the current generation, no man will pass on the pain to his children.

Producing wildlife for economic reasons would make huge sense for our country. While it will create the stakes of the local communities in conservation, it will also attract private capital into conservation related businesses. Most of the livestock ranches in Africa have converted into private game parks because the profits from hunting, tourism and the sale of live animals to other businesses are more than those from producing milk and beef. This has added millions of hectares of wild land to government owned wilderness, generating huge ecological dividends. While we are imbibing so much from other countries in this globalised world, what is stopping us from learning successful conservation from successful models abroad? It is just the mind-set, stupid!

4

Wildlife Tourism: A Conservation Tool

Panna National Park was created in 1981, and I became its first director in 1982. I remember laughing when, after going round the park, someone had asked me, "But where is the park?" As many Indians had no idea back then that a forest can also be a place for enjoyment, those who saw the sign board of a "national park" innocently expected it to be a big place with flower beds and fountains. Slightly more enlightened people thought we were going to bring tigers and other animals from outside for the benefit of white tourists. For them, the only purpose of having wild animals was to promote tourism in the area. However, like most of my ilk, I continued to believe that the primary purpose of having national parks was to preserve wildlife for some higher purpose, and tourism was only incidental. Only now I realise how right those innocent people were, even in that age! The original idea of a national park, in fact, was to preserve nature and wild animals primarily for people to watch and enjoy. That is why these areas are called "parks".

Americans created the first national parks, Yellowstone and Yosemite, in the late nineteenth century. Yellowstone was meant to be a "public park or pleasuring-ground for the benefit and enjoyment of the people" and, similarly, Yosemite was created "for public use, resort and recreation". All other nations borrowed the idea of national parks from the Americans, and the national parks that followed became famous attractions for visitors in all continents. Although the WLPA does not expressly say that the national parks were meant for the enjoyment of the people, it does allow people to visit our parks for the purpose of "photography" and "tourism". Our national parks and wildlife sanctuaries are meant for "the purpose of protecting, propagating and developing wildlife or its environment." However, one of the only two primary objectives of a national park, as per IUCN definition, by which every nation swears is "to promote education and recreation". Thus, tourism is a natural concomitant of wildlife conservation. The world over, wildlife and tourism are considered two sides of the same coin. Governments preserve wild animals so that people can watch them. If they have wild animals and wild landscapes, they want people to come and watch them.

Wildlife Tourism and the National Tiger Conservation Authority

In India, wildlife tourism is virtually synonymous with tiger tourism, as nearly all well-known protected areas (national parks and wildlife sanctuaries) are tiger reserves too. Although many of the tiger reserves also support other charismatic species like elephants and rhinos, a visit to a tiger reserve is always incomplete without seeing the tiger. Although tourism in all tiger reserves is growing, the growth in some high profile tiger reserves has been quite spectacular in recent year. Rather than trying to find ways of harnessing the benefits of this growth for conservation and communities, the GoI has been trying to stop all tourism in protected areas. Since its creation in 2006, the National Tiger Conservation Authority (NTCA), which has been empowered to issue directions to any "person, officer or authority" for the preservation of tigers in the country and to "lay down normative standards for tourism" under the WLPA, has been issuing advisories to the states to phase out tourism from all protected areas.

The first such signal came in the form of "Revised Guidelines For The Ongoing Centrally Sponsored Scheme Of Project Tiger - February, 2008" where it stated that "The core/critical tiger habitats would not be used for any form of tourism, and the ongoing tourism activities in such areas should be phased out in the fringe/buffer areas, without affecting its corridor value." Thereafter, the NTCA circulated for comments several versions of "Forest and Wildlife Ecotourism" guidelines to the states, in many of which they advocated the "phasing out" of ecotourism from the core areas and other national parks and sanctuaries. MP strongly opposed this approach. Perhaps because it did not get any support from the states, the NTCA had discontinued the emphasis on phasing out tourism in the later versions of its guidelines. However, it reverted to its original chant as soon as it saw an opportunity of its enforcement through a court order. A public interest litigation (Writ Petition No. 12351/2010, Ajay Dubey vs. National Tiger Conservation Authority and Others), praying for the enforcement of the NTCA's guidelines on wildlife tourism, was filed in the High Court of Madhya Pradesh at Jabalpur. Although the NTCA supported the petition, on January 2011 the high court rejected the demand for a stay on tourism in protected areas.

The case landed in the Supreme Court {S.L.P. (CIVIL) No. 21339 of 2011, Ajay Dubey vs. Union of India and Others}. Even before going into the merits of the application, the court, on 24th July 2012, got peeved at some peripheral issues and imposed an interim ban on all tourism in the core areas until, among other things, GoI issued proper guidelines for regulating tourism in tiger reserves. Again agreeing with the petitioner, the NTCA submitted a set of draft guidelines to the court which provided for phasing out tourism from PAs in five years. However, the NTCA was forced to retract its draft guidelines, under huge public pressure, on the next hearing on 22nd August, 2012, saying that they no longer wanted to ban tourism altogether because "The States have expressed concern that many local people depend on tourism for their livelihood and hence stoppage of tourism .... may be a threat to wildlife and forests ...." and that "the common citizen would be deprived of an opportunity to appreciate our natural heritage." The ban was lifted by the court on 16th October, 2012, after the GoI/NTCA notified another version of their guidelines on tourism in core areas. These guidelines allow tourism in the core areas of tiger reserves but under very severe restrictions (discussed later in this chapter).

These guidelines (NTCA 2012), although seen by many as a U-turn by the NTCA and MoEFCC in favour of wildlife tourism, unmistakably convey the impression that they are committed to stifling tourism in protected areas, even though they have been unable to stop it this time. The guidelines provide that tourism in tiger reserves shall be allowed only within miniscule "tourism zones", which cannot be increased in the future, and in miniscule numbers, calculated according to a dodgy formula (see discussion later). The NTCA says that it favours "ecotourism" and "low-impact wildlife tourism" but does not see ecotourism as anything beyond safari drives, and they propose impact reduction by reducing tourism influx alone. In fact, it forbade all states from allowing tourist walks in tiger reserves when we launched a novel low-impact tourism scheme called "Patrolling the Tiger Land" to allow tourists to join forest patrols, for a fee, in 2010.

Interestingly, the guidelines also provide that "Contravention of any provision of these guidelines or conditions laid therein by any person or organization shall be liable of (*sic*) an offence under sub-section (2) of 38-O of the Wild Life (Protection) Act, 1972," which means at least three years in jail. Obviously, these are not just guidelines to help the field agencies; they are, rather, *the law* now.

India must be the only country in the world where tourism and conservation of wildlife are considered incompatible and where the government is allowing wildlife tourism only under duress. This is despite the fact that the National Wildlife Action Plan (2002-2016) calls tourism a "vital conservation tool". WLPA allows people to enter PAs for the purpose of "photography" and "tourism" as mentioned before, and the local authorities, through Tiger Conservation Foundations, are required by law to "promote ecotourism" in tiger reserves. Why NTCA does not like wildlife tourism, despite clear legal and policy backing, has never been explained, either to the states or to the general public.

Wildlife Tourism and the Law

That tourism is an integral part of conservation is an established fact, as it enhances the security of animals and creates jobs for people. Why the Government of India, through NTCA, was keen to ban tourism in protected areas is totally inexplicable, although the unthinkable was being purportedly done in the name of some dubious provisions of the Wild Life (Protection) Act, 1972 (WLPA). Therefore, no discussion on wildlife tourism in India can be complete without an understanding of these provisions.

The WLPA has several references, direct or indirect, to tourism, namely:

a.   Section 28 authorises the CWLW, who can delegate this power to other officers as well, to issue permits to "enter or reside" in a protected area for purposes of "photography" and "tourism", among other things;

b.   Section 33 vests the CWLW with the responsibility to "control, manage and maintain" all protected areas and authorises him to "take such measures, in the interest of wild life, as he may consider necessary", but it forbids the "construction of commercial tourist lodges, hotels, zoos and safari parks" inside PAs without the "prior approval of the National Board";

c. Section 38-O (a) empowers the NTCA to "approve the Tiger Conservation Plan" for tiger reserves. Proposals for tourism must, naturally, be embedded in these plans;

d. Section 38-O (c) empowers the NTCA to "lay down normative standards for tourism activities .... in the buffer and core areas of tiger reserves and ensure their due compliance";

e. Section 38-X (2) (b) authorises the Tiger Conservation Foundations, which are headed by the Field Directors of the reserves, "to *promote* eco-tourism .... in the tiger reserves".

f. Above all, section 38-O (2) empowers the NTCA to "issue directions -- to any person, officer or authority for the protection of tiger, tiger reserve and such person, officer or authority shall be bound to comply with the directions".

It is clear that under the law the CWLW and the NTCA both have the responsibility to regulate tourism in protected areas. While CWLW is the sole authority for ordinary sanctuaries and national parks, the ones which happen to be part of the tiger reserves are subject to directions from both the offices. Although the law does not specify any hierarchy in such matters, the management of these areas is now almost entirely controlled by NTCA, and the position of the CWLW is reduced to merely implementing the NTCA directives.

However, the provision that the NTCA was ostensibly using to ban or curb tourism in tiger reserves has no reference to tourism per se. NTCA was using the definition of the "core area," also called the "critical tiger habitat", given in section 38-V of WLPA to justify its stand on tourism in tiger reserves. As per the definition of a tiger reserve given in the Explanation under section 38-V, a tiger reserve consists of:

a.   **a core area** or a critical tiger habitat situated within a wildlife sanctuary or a national park, which is "required to be kept as *inviolate* for the purposes of tiger conservation";

b.   **a buffer zone** peripheral to the core area where "a lesser degree of habitat protection is required to ensure the integrity of the critical tiger habitat ...."

The NTCA, somehow, believes that the word "inviolate" used in the definition of the "core area" means that these areas are to be kept free from all human activity, including tourism, although the Act unequivocally mandates the local authorities to promote ecotourism in tiger reserves. Therefore, tourism per se cannot be a violation of the inviolate area. As this word (inviolate) is not defined in the Act, it is subject to various interpretations and NTCA has chosen to interpret it in its own way. The online dictionary Encarta describes the word as "unaltered", "kept pure", "unable to be attacked or harmed", "something that is inviolate cannot be attacked or harmed", etc. It is quite obvious that to make the core areas inviolate, the state has to ensure that any activities that can *harm* the core area must be prevented. Such activities can possibly be of two kinds. Firstly, the activities or actions which are specifically described as *violations* in the WLPA, such as illegal hunting of wild animals, destruction of a wildlife habitat, etc. Secondly, those activities which are not prohibited by the Act but can still impact the core area or its wild animals adversely if not carefully managed and regulated. While the first category of activities, i.e. the offences, have to be prevented outright, the second category will need to be regulated, modified or prohibited, as the case may be, in order to eliminate or mitigate the impact on a case to case basis. As tourism is a legitimately permitted activity under section 28 and section 38-X of the Act, it can only come under the second category, i.e. there can be no blanket ban on tourism but its impact should be examined on a case to case basis and suitable steps taken to mitigate any perceived or visible, existing or potential, adverse impact.

It is important to note that even the amended WLPA endows the tiger reserves with no special sanctity beyond what was already available to the national parks and sanctuaries which form the core areas of all reserves. What is an offence in the core area of a tiger reserve is also an offence in ordinary PAs. Too much importance is being given by the NTCA, to the word "inviolate" used in the context of the tiger reserves, inexplicably ignoring the fact that the law had already provided — even before the expression "tiger reserve" was coined — the framework for making all protected areas inviolate by providing for the "extinction" and "acquisition" of *all private rights* in national parks and sanctuaries {WLPA sections 24 and 35 (4)}.

Although common people think that only the core areas of tiger reserves are meant to be made "inviolate", The Scheduled Tribes And Other Traditional Forest Dwellers (Recognition Of Forest Rights) Act, 2006 (FRA 2006) clearly recognises the intention of WLPA to make *all* sanctuaries and national parks inviolate by introducing the concept of "critical wild life habitats", which, as per this Act, are such areas of national parks and sanctuaries that are "required to be kept as *inviolate* for the purposes of wild life conservation". The words used to describe the "critical tiger habitat" and the "critical wild life habitat" in the two laws are exactly the same. Therefore, if making an area inviolate means stopping tourism as well, then it will equally apply to all sanctuaries and national parks, not only to tiger reserves. This contention is obviously untenable as such a situation will be utterly illogical and suicidal. Moreover, such a move will also be illegal as the law clearly mandates the authorities with the responsibility "to promote eco-tourism .... in tiger reserves"{section 38-X (2) (b)}.

The NTCA often claims that it is prohibiting tourism only in the core areas of tiger reserves, not from the buffer zones. This may appeal to the lay public who think that the core area is some small part of the tiger reserve while, for all intents and purposes, the core area is the *real* tiger reserve. The buffer zone is only a supportive envelope. The core areas are hundreds of square kilometres of national parks or wildlife sanctuaries which people have been traditionally coming to see. No one wants to pay for visiting the buffer zone of a tiger reserve, which often has nothing but cattle and dung to show.

Although the case for banning tourism is still pending with the Supreme Court, it is quite clear by now that tourism is not an illegal activity in tiger reserves or other protected areas. By issuing the latest guidelines, the NTCA seems to have accepted that there is no need to "phase out" tourism from protected areas.

Why Tourism in Protected Areas

Wild animals look beautiful and exciting in their natural habitats, and people feel pleasure in watching them in nature. A visit to a wilderness lends one a feeling of peace or adventure, depending upon what one is seeking from the experience. If for nothing else, the government is duty bound to facilitate the access of the public to wild areas, namely, national parks and sanctuaries, just for this reason. It is a service which the public demands and the government is obliged to provide.

On top of that, wildlife tourism renders several important services to conservation, local communities and the society at large. It helps in building a conservation-conscious constituency in the public, generates financial and non-financial resources for strengthening conservation, and creates great economic benefits for the society. Although no human endeavour comes without its side effects, the benefits of tourism to conservation and society far outweigh its potential adverse impacts as briefly discussed below.

As the creation of earning opportunities for the people and the preservation of the environment are the primary responsibilities of a government, any endeavour can be considered desirable if:

a.   it generates social, economic, spiritual or any other kind of benefits for the public;
b.   it conserves the natural environment; and
c.   its impact, if any, on the society or environment is acceptable, especially vis a vis the benefits.

Wildlife tourism is a part of the larger concept popularly called *ecotourism*, which was defined by The International Ecotourism Society (TIES) in 1990 as *"responsible travel to natural areas that conserves the environment and improves the well-being of local people"*. TIES further explains that "Ecotourism is about *uniting conservation, communities, and sustainable travel.* This means that those who implement and participate in ecotourism activities should follow the following ecotourism principles:

• Minimize impact.
• Build environmental and cultural awareness and respect.
• Provide positive experiences for both visitors and hosts.
• Provide direct financial benefits for conservation.
• Provide financial benefits and empowerment for local people.

- Raise sensitivity to host countries "political, environmental, and social climate."

(https://www.ecotourism.org/book/ecotourism-definition)

Obviously, wildlife tourism would be desirable if it meets even one of these criteria, i.e. conservation of environment and improvement in the well-being of the local people. However, tourism may become undesirable if its impact on either the environment or on the people is beyond acceptable limits, even if its benefits to either or both the entities are significant. In such a situation, either the activity has to be modified to reduce the impact to acceptable levels or, in extreme cases, it has to be banned altogether.

Economic Power of Travel and Tourism

That travel and tourism is one of the biggest generators of wealth and jobs in the world is universally recognised; therefore, its value for human welfare is unquestionable. The 2014 edition of the UNWTO Tourism Highlights has come up with the following estimates for tourism in 2013

Table 2: UNWTO Tourism Highlights 2014.

Contribution to global Gross Domestic Product (GDP)	9%
Creation of Jobs	One in 11 (9%)
Value of Exports	$14 trillion (6% of World's Exports
Total International Exports	1087 million
Domestic Travellers	5-6 billion
International Arrivals in India	6.85 million
Foreign Exchange Receipts by India	$18.40 billion

According to the World Travel and Tourism Council's research report entitled "WTTC Travel and Tourism Economic Impact 2014", the contribution of travel and tourism to the economy of the world in 2013 is summed up as follows:

Table 3: WTTC Travel and Tourism Highlights 2014

Item	World	India
GDP: Direct Contribution	$2,155.4 billion (2.9% of total)	INR 2178 billion (2% of total)
GDP: Total Contribution	$69,990.3 billion (9.5% of total)	INR 6631 billion (6.2%)
Employment: Direct Contribution	100,894,000 jobs (3.4% of total)	22,320,000 jobs (4.9% of total)
Employment: Total Contribution	265,855,000 jobs (8.9% of Total)	35,438,500 jobs (7.7% of total)
Visitor Exports	$1,295.9 billion (5.4% of total exports)	INR 1,110 billion (4.1%)
Investments	$754.6 billion (4.4% of total)	INR 1,938 billion (6.2%)

According to the WTTC (2013), "The Travel and Tourism industry in India is almost three times bigger than the automotive manufacturing industry and generates more jobs than the chemical manufacturing, automotive manufacturing, communications and mining sectors added together." The report further says that:

• Travel and Tourism's total contribution – including direct, indirect and induced impacts – to GDP in India was around 6.4% of the total GDP. This compares to 3.3% of automotive manufacturing, 4.5% of education and 3.7% of mining industry.

- Supporting 39 million direct, indirect and induced jobs in India, Travel and Tourism generates more jobs than the mining industry and communication services.

- US$ one million spent on Travel and Tourism in India generates $1.3 million worth in GDP, which is greater than the agriculture, automotive and chemicals industry. This amount supports 407 jobs, which is more than the average of communication services (381 jobs), financial services (329 jobs), manufacturing (315 jobs) and chemicals (231 jobs).

- Tourism is one of the major export sectors of developing countries and is the primary source of foreign exchange earnings in 46 of the 49 Least Developed Countries. Tourism is a crucial contributor to these countries" income – up to 70% for the world's poorest countries.

Tourism is included in the Poverty Reduction Strategies of more than 80% of low income countries (CREST: Responsible Travel: Global Trends & Statistics).

Perhaps we need no more evidence to corroborate the value of tourism for the creation of wealth and jobs for human welfare.

Economic Power of Ecotourism

Although all jobs created by tourism should be welcome, jobs in the remote areas where the most deprived people live and eke out a living by overexploiting depleting natural resources are even more precious. These jobs are created by ecotourism, nature tourism or wildlife tourism — whatever name we give it — and reduce the pressure on natural resources. Nature tourism or ecotourism is an important component of the global leisure tourism activity and is growing much faster than general tourism. Although estimates of the market size of nature tourism or ecotourism vary, all estimates tell us that nature tourism is a very significant component of the overall travel market As per Ceballos Lascurains, (1993), nature tourism generates 7% of all international travel expenditure, while according to another estimate (Fillion et al, 1992), 40-60% of all international tourists are nature tourists and 20-40% are wildlife tourists, including bird watchers. While overall tourism has historically grown at about 4% per annum, on average nature tourism has grown at approximately 10% to 30% (WTO 1993). Obviously, the jobs created by ecotourism, primarily in the remote areas, are also growing significantly.

There are a variety of reports that highlight the economic impact of ecotourism in specific locations. Some examples of such studies are given below:

- Kruger National Park in South Africa received nearly a million visitors in 2002, and the jobs it supported were estimated at 60,000 direct jobs and 300,000-500,000 indirect jobs (Chelsea 2008).

- As per the Department of Fish and Wildlife, in the state of Washington, USA, the number of jobs created by the "watchable wildlife industry" is estimated at 21,000, which is second only to Boeing and is 5.2 times more than Microsoft's jobs in the state. Wildlife watching creates an economic boost to the state's economy that is nearly double that of the state's biggest agricultural commodity, apples.

- 1.3 million visitors to the Mount Rainier National Park in Washington generated $9.0 million in personal incomes for local residents and supported 649 local jobs, and another $3.9 million in personal incomes and 163 jobs through the "multiplier effect" (Sun *et al.* 2002).

- Olympic National Park in the same state hosted 3.3 million recreation visits in 2000. Park visitors spent $90 million in the local area, generating $29 million in direct personal income (wages and salaries) for local residents and supporting 1,900 jobs in tourism businesses. Tourism accounts for about 10% of area employment (Stynes *et al.* 2001).

- Wildlife watching people spent $54.9 billion and hunters and anglers spent another $89.8 billion in 2007 in pursuit of their interests in the USA (2011 National Survey of Fishing, Hunting And Wildlife-Associated Recreation, USFWS and Census Bureau USA).

- In an example quoted in the "Economic Values of Protected Areas" (IUCN), visitor expenditure in the "Federal Interest Lands" in South Florida created 3440 local jobs, while the government expenditure on the these lands funded another 1341 jobs.

Although, in view of the complexities of the travelling activity, it is virtually impossible to quantify the impact of tourism on local economies accurately, some intelligent guess work can easily bring home the point, even to a layman. It is simple to understand that when people travel, they spend money to buy goods and services and create jobs which run households, put food on the table and send children to schools. Therefore, the volume of jobs created by tourism depends on how much money people spend while travelling. An important point to bear in mind is that all production of goods and services is ultimately dependent on the "low-end" jobs for primary production, although it may not be obvious to a casual observer. Even if a large salary is paid to a lodge manager, he will have to use this money to buy goods and services he needs to run his household. This will create jobs for the low end workers at the final stage, either for growing the food the family consumes or for its transportation or for packaging or paying the delivery boy and so on. Therefore, the circulation of money spent by visitors ultimately creates employment opportunities for the poorest people somewhere along the supply chain, although the visitor may be paying it to a rich lodge owner.

A million visitors to Kruger National Park in South Africa have been estimated by experts to produce approximately one job per two or three visitors, as mentioned before. Using the same logic, it is interesting to estimate the job creation potential of the protected areas in MP. The state received 1,109,048 Indian visits and 92,298 visits from overseas guests in all its parks between July 2010 and June 2011. Although we do not know how the Kruger study estimated the job creation, it is unlikely that so many jobs will be created per visitor by wildlife tourists in India as the bulk of the visitors are Indians — though from all parts of the country — while the visitors to African parks are overwhelmingly foreigners, who tend to spend more money. We have no data on how much these guests spend on their trips, but making some simple, conservative assumptions and using some common sense can show us the way. So, presuming that a family of four will have to spend on average approximately INR 10,000 ($166.67) on transportation between their home and the destination, INR 5000 per night on food and lodging and INR 5000 on two safaris in a typical park (including entry fee, guide fee and gypsy hire charges), one night's halt will produce eight person-safaris (two rounds for four persons each). Thus each entry into a park will cost the family INR 2500 ($41.67) per person, on an average. Extrapolating this to all the visits in 2010-11, the 1,201,346 visits must have produced an economy worth approximately INR 300.34 crore ($50.05 mn). Presuming a low-end job in India does not earn more than INR 50,000 per annum (Indian per capita income in 2010-11 was INR 53301 ($888.35) per annum), the total number of direct jobs created by the visitors should be approximately 60,000. Assuming a "multiplier effect" created by the circulation of primary money in the economy, at 1.5 the total number of jobs created by wildlife tourism comes to approximately 90,000. Although this is only a layman's guess, as I am not an economist, I think this should sum up the overall sense of the situation quite well until we have an expert analysis of the situation. Most of these jobs go to locals as local employees in wildlife lodges exceed 70% in most protected areas in the country (Karanth and DeFries 2010). These jobs must be a significant part of the total job market (approx. 0.75%) in the state, presuming one person in each of the approximately 12,000,000 families living in the state needs employment. Most of these jobs are created by the visitors to five tiger reserves of the state. The new guidelines on tourism in tiger reserves suddenly reduced these jobs to about 50%, rendering hundreds of young men jobless. Any government that renders so many people jobless should be held guilty of genocide, however pious the reasons may be behind such a policy.

These are only a few examples to illustrate how significant ecotourism or wildlife tourism is for job creation in the remote areas of the world. If any more proof is required to illustrate the economic relevance of ecotourism to local economies, a little search on the internet can provide much more material.

Tourism Saves Wild Animals and Wild Habitats

Although tourism does always have an impact on the values of protected areas visited by people, there is ample evidence globally that tourism confers more benefits on those areas than any harm caused by it, although the situation may vary from place to place, depending upon the quality of management and regulation. In an area managed for the preservation or production of wildlife, the ultimate criteria for judging the value of tourism must be the long-term trends in wildlife populations in the concerned area. If the populations of wild animals remain stable or increase, despite some possible ill effects of tourism, this alone should justify the promotion of wildlife tourism, if for nothing else. Similarly, if the desire of the states to promote tourism, for whatever reasons, brings more habitats under better protection, we cannot complain. There are numerous examples in the world proving that the advent of tourism, even hunting tourism, has resulted in the recovery of several endangered species of fauna and flora or has increased secure wildlife habitats. Some of these examples are briefly touched below:

1. The community-based natural resource management (CBNRM) programme sweeping Africa since the eighties, in which communities control and manage their natural resources outside national parks, has wildlife tourism, including trophy hunting, as its main driver.

Although economic gains to the individual members from CBNRM vary, as they depend upon several factors, one unequivocal gain from the programme has been that the wildlife populations have gone up quite significantly in areas covered by CBNRM. For example, the total population of all the mammals in the area managed by the Nyae Nyae conservancy in Namibia had grown to 14,000 by 2002 from an all-time low of less than 1,000 in the eighties (Weaver *et al.* 2003).

2. The population of the highly endangered mountain gorilla in the Virunga massif spread across Rwanda, Uganda and Congo grew from 380 to 480 in 7 years since 2003, mainly due to the "positive effect of gorilla tourism" and "integration of tourism and conservation". Tourists pay $500 for an hour of watching these animals in the national parks situated in the massif, and 5% of the revenue is spent on the communities surrounding the national parks (Jon Rosen, globalpost June 2010). A census of mountain gorillas showed a 17% increase in overall numbers between 1989 and 2000, and that the increase was greatest in gorilla groups habituated for tourism or for research. Tourism means that habituated groups are regularly visited and therefore receive greater protection than non-habituated groups (UNEP/CMS: Wildlife Watching and Tourism published in Imprint).

3. Península Valdés in Argentina is the nursery ground for one of the largest remaining

populations of southern right whales. This population has been studied since 1970 and now registers an annual growth of 7%. In 1991, around 17,400 people participated in boat-based whale watching; since then the participating number has grown at around 14% per year, and 96,400 passengers went on whale-watch tours at Península Valdés in 2004 (UNEP/CMS: Wildlife Watching and Tourism published in Imprint). This shows a clear interdependence between whales and tourism.

4.   As mentioned before, tourism and conservation have been intertwined ever since the very concept of conservation was born. National parks, the first of the modern protected areas, were primarily created by the Americans for protecting nature for the enjoyment of the people. The 1872 Act establishing the Yellowstone National Park, the first national park known to the modern world, describes the park as "....... the tract of land .... lying near the headwaters of the Yellowstone river .... is hereby reserved and withdrawn from settlement, occupancy or sale .... and dedicated and set apart as *a public park or pleasuring-ground for the benefit and enjoyment of the people* –." Similarly, the Yosemite National Park was conceived in the form of the "Yosemite Land Grant" in 1864 in the State of California by the President "upon the express conditions that the premises shall be held for public use, resort, and recreation [and] shall be inalienable for all time."

Obviously, wild animals residing in these parks have benefited from the desire of the people to see them and have prospered there. These lands would have been long gone if the American people did not have a strong love of the wilds.

5.   In a comprehensive anthology, aptly entitled the "Positive Effects of Wildlife Tourism on Wildlife", K. Higginbottom *et al.* (2010) say that wildlife tourism can help conservation of wildlife in four ways: (1) financial contributions, (2) non-financial contributions, (3) socio-economic incentives, and (4) education. While the financial contributions by way of entrance fees and tourist donations, etc. help meet deficits in government finances available for the management of protected areas, the non-financial contributions accrue through the participation of tourists and operators in conservation work such as research and monitoring. The socioeconomic incentives created by wildlife tourism for conservation motivate private and public agencies to maintain and restore wildlife habitats with an eye on commercial benefits. The educational effect of wildlife tourism enhances visitor awareness of conservation related issues and encourages them to behave in a manner that has positive consequences for animals or their habitats.

6.   The Higginbottom report gives several examples of protected areas in Australia, created primarily with the objective of promoting tourism as a means of socioeconomic upliftment of the concerned regions. It says that at least 15

protected areas in Australia, such as Barron Grounds Nature Reserve (NSW), Montague Island Nature Reserve (NSW), Fogg Dam Conservation Reserve (NT), etc. have been created for attracting tourism for its economic benefits. The following excerpt from the report highlights the contribution of wildlife tourism to enhancing the wildlife habitats in private lands:

"In a survey of 27 private game reserves in the province of KwaZulu-Natal, 48% of managers said that if they had not had (wildlife) tourism available as an alternative commercial option, they would have continued to farm cattle (generally considered to be a less sustainable land use than wildlife viewing in such areas) (James and Goodman 2000). The authors also concluded that nature tourism was responsible for reintroduction of popular game viewing species such as lion, cheetah, elephant and buffalo; a wider distribution of other animal species; and an increase in "connectivity" of wildlife habitats across the broader landscape. Across the whole of South Africa, successful reintroduction programs on hundreds of private game reserves and small state reserves are reported to have been motivated largely by the economic incentive provided by wildlife tourism, especially wildlife viewing. Similarly in Namibia, the financial returns from wildlife on private lands (40-45% of which was attributed to tourism) doubled between 1972 and 1996, motivating a trend toward conversion of private land from livestock to wildlife (Richardson 1998). Another study showed that non-consumptive wildlife viewing in Namibia yielded the highest net economic return out of various land use options (Barnes and de Jager 1996). Other international examples described by Buckley and Sommer (2001) illustrate that the financial benefits derived from nature-based tourism (including wildlife tourism) can be used to support management of private lands for conservation -- though it is unclear to what extent this would have occurred in the absence of tourism. In Europe, there are large private estates including areas of conservation significance that effectively operate as private tourism ventures. In many Latin American countries, there are private lands purchased for conservation purposes and financially supported by tourism. In North America, many private lands are managed in a relatively undisturbed state for recreational hunting."

7.   In India, although the protected areas are technically the properties of the states, most of the funding for managing these areas, other than staff salaries, comes from the central government. There are 102 national parks and 515 wildlife sanctuaries in the country, and the grants available from the central government are always inadequate for effective protection and management, although the 41 tiger reserves do get a disproportionately high share of the

available funds. The Ministry of Environment, Forests and Climate Change (MoEFCC) disbursed an amount of INR 56.52 crore ($9.43 mn) and the NTCA gave away another INR 144.99 crore ($24.16 mn) to all the 617 protected areas in the country, i.e. an average of INR 32,60,000 ($54,333) per PA in the financial year 2011-12. In fact, the bulk of the PAs, outside the tiger reserves, only got a measly one million rupees (less than $20,000). Against this, Madhya Pradesh alone earned a sum of INR 15.41 crore ($2.57 mn) from wildlife tourism and spent it on its 34 protected areas, at an average of INR 44.0 lakh ($73,333) per PA (2010-11). Madhya Pradesh has been spending all its tourism revenue on the parks themselves since 1997. Obviously, the tourism revenues are a major source of sustenance for the protected areas in states like MP. Although MP got INR 45.957 crore ($7.66 mn) in 2011-12 from GoI and NTCA, our own earnings from tourism also rose to a significant sum of approximately INR 200 million in the 2011-12 tourism year (July to June). The Bandhavgarh Tiger Reserve alone received $1.2 million in tourist revenue and almost the same amount from government sources (Buckley and Pabla 2012). Obviously, without tourism revenues, PAs in MP would have been in a far worse condition.

8.   Tourism revenue is critical for the maintenance of PAs, wherever such revenues are significant, for several reasons. Madhya Pradesh is one state where tourism revenues of some PAs have become substantial over the last few years and the state allows them to spend this income on park management and local communities. Apart from making up the deficit in government funding, these funds are especially important as these are available to the PA managers at the beginning of the year while regular budget from the state and the centre takes several months to materialise. Although the financial systems in the state have become quite efficient in the last few years, the central funds are still not available for expenditure before September, while the second instalment can rarely be utilised as it is available only by March. As a result, the PA managers have to depend upon their own resources, i.e. the park revenues, to meet the expenses for most of the year, even if some of the expenses may be recouped when the central funds arrive. In case these funds were not available, the abilities of the managers to patrol and maintain the parks would be seriously crippled, especially in the first six months of the year.

9.   Equally importantly, the parks are also able to do several things with the tourism revenues for which regular funds are not available. For example, MP has been able to reintroduce tigers

in Panna, gaur in Bandhavgarh, and blackbuck in Kanha only because we had access to this source of funding. If we had had to depend upon regular government funding, it would have been virtually impossible to undertake such path-breaking initiatives, as the governments are perpetually in the austerity mode.

With the recent reduction in funding for the forestry sector under the new government, the need for self-reliance has further been underlined. Recourse to sustainable tourism in PAs can help move in that direction.

10. Apart from generating funds for conservation, tourism helps wildlife in several other ways as well. Poachers and other criminals are likely to avoid well-visited areas for fear of being seen by visitors, at least during the daytime. Visitors do act as extra ears and eyes for the conservation agencies. I personally know of at least three cases, two in Kanha and one in Bandhavgarh, where visitors informed the authorities of having seen tigers carrying wire snares around their necks or gin traps on their feet In all three cases, we were able to remove the snares/traps and save the tigers. Tourism zones are also better supervised and, as a result, are better patrolled by the staff. An obvious indicator of the contribution of tourism in conservation is that wildlife has survived only in a few well-visited parks in the country. Even in these parks, the highest wildlife densities are generally seen only in tourism zones. One can reason that animals

have survived in these areas because more resources are spent on protection of tourism zones, not because of tourism per se, but more resources are directed at these areas primarily because these areas are our showcases. Although the resources that are available to some high profile protected areas — mainly tiger reserves — have increased significantly in the last few years, the animals have survived the deficient years in these areas primarily because these areas were under the public gaze through tourism. In the absence of tourism, these areas would perhaps have been no different from the millions of hectares of other forests without any worthwhile wildlife presence. Until recently, even the well-known PAs were not as well funded as a normal territorial division. While wildlife has generally declined in all territorial forests, it has survived in PAs, especially in those which were known for their tourism. Somehow, there is a clear connection between wild animals and tourism: they sustain each other!

Adverse Impacts of Tourism

Of course, nothing comes free of cost and tourism is no exception. Tourism does have its adverse impacts, both on communities and wildlife. Habituation of animals to human presence, garbage, overcrowding, accidents, cultural contamination of local communities, disruption of wildlife corridors due to infrastructure development, etc. are the common impacts of wildlife tourism, although their intensity varies from place to place, depending upon visitor volumes and quality of management.

- Habituation of animals to human presence has its disadvantages as well as advantages. Habituated animals are easily seen and photographed, leading to better visitor satisfaction, and the animals feel no stress or discomfort in human presence. Intimate interaction with habituated animals like patting, hand-feeding, etc. may result in disease communication and accidents. However, it is common knowledge that habituated animals, like tigers in India and gorillas in Congo and Rwanda, live longer and breed better than other animals. This may be because the presence of visitors improves the security environment around them. Moreover, these animals are monitored by the regular visitors, guides and drivers, and, if a particular animal is not seen for some time, visitors want answers from the authorities. Sometime ago, when the famous B-1 tiger of Bandhavgarh was not seen for some time, there was a serious buzz in the media and the authorities had to mount a search, which resulted in the discovery of its dead body a few kilometres outside the park.

- Garbage inside the PAs does not seem to be much of a problem now, except in places of mass tourism around religious and picnicking sites situated inside PAs. Wildlife tourists are generally more sensitive to the garbage issue, and most of our parks are now absolutely free from garbage. However, garbage, including human excreta, continues to be a serious problem in places like Pachmarhi, especially at the time of festivals when thousands of pilgrims converge on this otherwise pristine hill station. In any case, this kind of tourism is not the subject of debate in the general context of wildlife management, as it is limited to a few sites in the country. Garbage generated by visitors, their commercial hosts and service providers, particularly outside PAs, is a serious concern and needs to be dealt with by the local civic bodies.

- Overcrowding of sensitive sites and areas is the commonly seen impact of heavy visitation in some Indian parks. Pictures of several vehicles jostling for the best view of a tiger walking on the road in Corbett, Bandhavgarh, Kanha and Ranthambhore, have been used by the critics of tourism to strengthen their position. Efforts at reducing such overcrowding through the imposition of a carrying capacity sub-division of the tourism zones into sub-zones and establishment of route systems have made only a limited impact, primarily for two reasons. Firstly, the eagerness of the drivers to please their guests, for whom seeing a tiger in the wild may be a once in a lifetime experience. Secondly, the limited number of entry and exit points and fixed timings for entry and exit is a sure recipe for overcrowding. As all the vehicles enter and exit from the parks at the same time from only one or two gates, they have to travel together for some distance till they reach a point where the routes separate. And many of them over-speed to beat the clock on their return. Perhaps having multiple entry points and staggered entry and exit timings can help in mitigating this problem to some extent, if the tourism zone cannot be enlarged. However, if the tourism zones are enlarged, along with multiple gates and free timings for entry and exit, the problem can be completely eliminated.

- Along with overcrowding of some parks, disruption of wildlife corridors around the same parks, due to the construction of lodges, is the second most vicious criticism which wildlife tourism has to contend with. Prerna Singh Bindra's "Report on impact of tourism on tigers and other wildlife in Corbett Tiger Reserve" brought the problem into national and international focus. Although the problem is serious in some cases, the way it is portrayed by the critics makes it look as if wildlife lodges are the only culprits constricting wildlife corridors and habitats while, in fact, the real issue is the expansion of human habitats into wildlife habitats everywhere. Appropriate action must be taken against any lodges indulging in any illegal practices, and they should be suitably counselled if any of their practices are unsustainable or do not go well with the overall character of the place even if they are not illegal. But to portray that only the lodges come in the way of animal movements between the parks and the surrounding forests, while villages and towns around them are expanding relentlessly, is like missing the woods for the trees. In any case, these lodges are built on private, cultivated or wooded lands. The poor owners of these lands are well within their rights to maximize their benefits by selling or leasing the lands to commercial lodges under the prevailing laws. Perhaps we can bring in laws, if need be, for restricting the use of any more lands for building lodges, though at a tremendous cost to the local people. A more prudent approach, however, would be to incentivize appropriate land uses or to acquire certain critical patches of private lands for merger with the parks. A good wildlife lodge adjoining a park, without a fence and with sufficient open spaces, is a much more wildlife-friendly land use than agriculture. No farmer wants wild animals on his land while the lodges are dying to have animals roaming on their premises.

• Accidents do happen, though rarely, due to overcrowding and over-speeding by tourist vehicles. At least two tigers have been killed in collision with tourist vehicles in Bandhavgarh — one in 2009 and another in 2010. Once a tiger jumped over a jeep and mauled a visitor in Bandhavgarh when its way was blocked by a train of vehicles, perhaps in 2002. One kitchen worker was killed by a tiger at Dhikala in Corbett National Park at night some time ago. Although the incidence of accidents can certainly be reduced to some extent through better regulation and education, stray accidents can never be ruled out, even under the best management.

- Some influence of distant or alien cultures on locals is inevitable, but all of us will perhaps never agree whether such influences are good or bad. Cultures do change and evolve with time, and an interaction between locals and visitors is just another part of this process of cultural evolution.

These impacts of tourism on wildlife and people are real but are not so serious as to warrant a complete ban or a serious curb on tourism in protected areas, as many of them can be significantly mitigated through proper management and regulation. Despite these impacts — potential as well as real — wildlife tourism does help conservation as well as communities significantly, making it one of the principal tools for conservation and rural development in most countries. As every human activity has an impact on the environment, human progress has to go on while keeping these impacts to the minimum, rather than abandoning progress completely. The move by the Government of India, through the NTCA, first to outlaw wildlife tourism completely and then to seriously curb it defies logic in every way. The guidelines issued by the NTCA under the direction of the Supreme Court are going to have a profound effect on the future of wildlife tourism in India. Therefore, it is important to examine these guidelines critically in any discussion on wildlife tourism in the country.

Tourism in Tiger Reserves

As discussed before, tourism in tiger reserves is allowed only in accordance with the guidelines issued by the NTCA in 2012 under the direction of the Supreme Court of India. The exact title of the guidelines is not clear as the subject of the circular dated 15 October, 2012, which issued the document to the state CWLWs, calls them the "Comprehensive Guidelines for tiger conservation and tourism as provided under section 38 O (1) (c) of the Wild Life (Protection) Act, 1972", while the draft gazette notification attached with the circular gives the title as "National Tiger Conservation Authority (Normative Standards for Tourism activities and Project Tiger) Guidelines, 2012". "Guidelines for Tourism in and Around Tiger Reserves" are given in Part B of this notification. This document seems to be one of the worst examples of poor drafting and poor knowledge of the subject on which these sweeping guidelines have been issued for compliance by the entire country. Although the document has been issued only in the form of guidelines, in fact its compliance is mandatory as the violation of any of its provisions is an offence under section 38-O (2) of WLPA. The document makes all the usual sweet statements in favour of ecotourism so that, if one is not aware of the background of these guidelines, one can be easily misled into believing that GoI and NTCA are strongly committed to promoting ecotourism as a conservation tool. But the meat of the document is extremely negative and has the potential of severely retarding the growth of ecotourism in the country.

Sifting through mostly irrelevant and insignificant matter, I was able to pick up the following salient features for discussion here:

a. Adopt ecotourism in place of wildlife tourism.

b. Ecotourism in tiger reserves should be community based and community driven.

c. Gate receipts shall be used for conservation and community support only.

d. Imposition of a conservation fee on the tourism industry for "ecodevelopment and local community upliftment works".

e. Constitution of a Local Advisory Committee (LAC) to "review" the tourism strategy of a tiger reserve and to "ensure computation" and "implementation" of "tiger reserve specific carrying capacity". The LAC will prescribe building norms for tourism facilities situated in the tiger reserve (i.e. buffer zones) and in the "zone of influence" of the tiger reserve and will monitor compliance with the legally mandated environmental norms and laws, and shall also monitor activities of tour operators.

f. No new tourism infrastructure shall be developed inside the core areas at all, and all existing residential accommodation shall be phased out.

g. Imposition of a carrying capacity limit on the number of vehicles and visitors (in non-vehicular activities).

h. Delineation of tourism zones in the core areas, subject to a limit of 20% of the total area or the existing area in use, whichever is less.

i.   Any core area in a tiger reserve from which relocation has been carried out shall not be used for developing tourism infrastructure.

j.   Tourism to be fostered in buffer zones and other peripheral areas.

k.   "Management of habitat to inflate animal abundance for tourism purposes shall not be practiced within the core or critical habitat."

l.   Contravention of the guidelines shall be an offence under subsection (2) of 38-O of the Wild Life (Protection) Act, 1972. (The simplest offence in a tiger reserve is punishable with *minimum* imprisonment for 3 years and a fine of INR 25000).

The Supreme Court order dated 16th October 2012 has directed that, "All the concerned authorities will ensure that the requirements in the aforesaid Guidelines for Tourism in and around the Tiger Reserves are complied with before tourism activities recommence" and vacated the stay order.

In some ways, these guidelines are better than the versions issued by the NTCA to the states earlier. At least the guidelines no longer want to phase out tourism from core areas, although states like Kerala had already converted those parts of the core areas into buffer zones where some of the finest tourism practices had been going on for several years.

The fundamental problem with these guidelines is that these are no longer mere guidelines. It is a very authoritarian diktat which must be obeyed by all, although compliance with all parts of the guidelines is impossible. As India is a very large and diverse country, no one straitjacket can fit the diversity of tourism opportunities, constraints and needs of all the tiger reserves in the country. We have small reserves and large reserves; old reserves with well-established tourism culture and new reserves with no tourism; areas with extensive road network and those with no road network at all; hilly areas, plains areas, marshy/aquatic tiger reserves (e.g. Sundarbans); reserves with only vehicular traffic (as in Ranthambhore, Corbett) and those with all non-vehicular traffic (e.g., Periyar); and so on. All these areas use different tourism practices. In Kanha, Corbett, etc. all the tourism is by vehicles; in Periyar it is all on foot or by cruise boats; in Sundarbans it is all by boats and launches. There is no way we can apply the same regulations to such varied practices. These guidelines are going to create serious problems in developing ecotourism as a tool for conservation and community development, which is the primary justification for allowing ecotourism in protected areas. Although these guidelines will seriously constrain ecotourism in existing destinations, the real impact will be on new protected areas where tourism development has been completely forbidden by these guidelines. Ideally, the states should be allowed and encouraged to develop their own ecotourism models based on local needs and opportunities. If issuing central guidelines is a must, which perhaps it is not, they should be only broad suggestions and expectations and must not be binding on the states.

Although most of the document consists of just sweet and innocuous statements, some features, such as limiting the tourism zones to less than 20%, and the imposition of an ultra-conservative carrying capacity, and banning the "management of habitat to inflate animal abundance for tourism purposes ...." are outright ridiculous. Limiting the tourism businesses only to community-based units will not help the communities in any way as most communities will not have the business acumen and marketing capacity required for creating a profitable business. "Imposition of a conservation fee on tourism industry" for "ecodevelopment and local community upliftment works" does sound very progressive but will be difficult to implement. No states are likely to come up with the necessary legislation anytime soon. On the contrary, raising the park fee is a much more convenient and effective way of raising extra resources for ecodevelopment. In any case, parks like Kanha, Pench and Bandhavgarh already spend a substantial part of their gate fees on local communities. Madhya Pradesh has been using its park revenues for conservation and community development since 1997. Now MP has made it mandatory to spend 25% of the park revenues on communities. Many other states are already in the process of creating similar systems, especially since the amended Act made it mandatory in 2006.

Banning any new tourism infrastructure, especially residential, inside the core area is logical, but concentrating tourism in only 20% or less of the area will concentrate such infrastructure into small belts around the parks, seriously impacting the so-called wildlife corridors. When the preamble to the guidelines says that *"Tourism in the form of ecotourism has the potential to enhance public awareness, education, and wildlife conservation, while providing nature-compatible local livelihoods and greater incomes for a large number of people living around natural ecosystem which can help to contribute directly to the protection of wildlife or forest areas, while making the local community stakeholders and owners in the process,"* restricting tourism to only 20% of the core area does not make sense. If ecotourism is so good for conservation and communities, the guidelines should have encouraged ecotourism everywhere. The guidelines do not explain why a cap of 20% is being imposed on the tourism zone or why the tourism zones cannot be increased to 20% if the current usage is less. It is not clear where this God-given number has come from. Despite concluding that in *"Current tourism zones .... tiger density and recruitment does not seem to be impacted,"* the guidelines go on to say, arbitrarily, that *"For this reason permitting up to 20% of the core/ critical tiger habitat as a tourism zone should not have an adverse effect on the tiger biology needs ...."* Obviously, the recommendation is contrary to the "reason" stated in the previous sentence. Equally inexplicably, the guidelines say that *"With this importance of tourism in tiger conservation in mind, it is recommended that a maximum of 20% of the core or critical tiger habitat usage (not exceeding the present usage) for regulated, low-impact tourist visitation may be permitted."* Obviously, if tourism is important, tourism zones should have been 20% or *more* of the available area, not the other way round. There is no indication why 20% is good and why 25% or 50% would have been deadly.

No one knows how this 20% is to be calculated. Visitors use only the space occupied by the infrastructure such as buildings, roads, trails, etc. It is not clear whether the tourism zone is the sum of the surface area of these structures or the area of the ranges, beats or compartments in which these facilities are situated. Whatever way one looks at it, this figure is ridiculous. The NTCA has perhaps recently clarified, again arbitrarily, that a belt of 20 metres on either side of the roads has to be added to the area of the roads to compute the area of the tourism zone. If that is the case, no tourism zone will be more than one or two percent of the total core area, but they cannot expand it to reach 20%.

The prescription that if the current usage is less than 20%, it cannot be increased to even 20% looks more and more ludicrous as one looks deeper. This means that the reserves where there is no or minimal tourism today cannot develop any tourism in the future, denying them and the neighbouring communities the benefits which these guidelines so emphatically claim to vouch for. What happens to the tiger reserves which are to be notified in the future? They will certainly be taken in on the condition that no tourism will be allowed in them. No state would offer its forests to NTCA in such a case if they have read these guidelines. The Government of MP has not approved the notification of the Ratapani sanctuary as a tiger reserve for the last five years, despite an in-principle approval from the NTCA, because the state is reluctant to invite the NTCA"s interference in any more areas in the state. This new provision will put the seal of finality on this stand of the state.

The prescription that the tourism zone should be reduced to 20% if it is more than the limit today is the height of arbitrariness. By reducing the area, we will either have to increase the impact per unit area — defeating the very purpose of these guidelines — or have to reduce the tourist intake. In either case it will be suicidal. If the reduction leads to a reduction in tourist intake, it will affect the jobs and businesses dependent on tourism, apart from reducing park revenues on which the security of the parks in states like MP depends so much. Destruction of people's legal livelihoods, for whatever reason, cannot be justified unless it is absolutely unavoidable. This move also seems to be in violation of the WLPA, which ordains that *"no such direction (regarding tiger conservation) shall interfere with or affect the rights of the local people, particularly the Scheduled Tribes"* {sec. 38-O (2)} and that the core areas have to be made inviolate only *"without affecting the rights of the Scheduled Tribes and such other forest dwellers ....*" *"{Explanation (i), sec. 38-V (4)}.* If making the core areas inviolate in this way means taking away the livelihoods of the local tribals and other communities, the law clearly forbids it.

Carrying Capacity

The regulation of tourist intake based on carrying capacity (CC) is another hallmark of these guidelines.

Although this provision sounds very progressive, in fact, it is one of the most retrograde features of these guidelines. The computation of the carrying capacity prescribed by these guidelines is an adaptation of the method used to calculate the carrying capacity of nature trails in Mexico (Ceballos-Lascurain 1992). The NTCA (Project Tiger) has been prescribing this methodology for computing the carrying capacity for safari vehicles in the reserves for several years, but no one took it seriously until it was packaged along with these guidelines. There are several serious flaws in this methodology. Firstly, the methodology is primarily applicable to *specific sites* such as trails, picnic sites, etc. within PAs, rather than to whole PAs. Secondly, it is applicable to static resources like natural scenery, while wildlife — especially species like tigers — are cryptic and mobile. People interested in watching wildlife tend to spend more time lingering in places where the chances of seeing a tiger or any other spectacular animal are higher. They also want to spend some time with the animals they see for photography, etc. Therefore, there is a natural tendency for the lumping together of safari vehicles. This is more a matter of regulation of traffic flow rather than computations. Thirdly, the original methodology envisages a continuous inflow of visitors during the day, while in most parks all the people get in virtually together and get out at the same time, as there are specific entry and exit times, generally twice a day.

Apart from these fundamental flaws, the way this methodology is applied is absolutely bizarre. In the Kanha model given in an annexure to the guidelines, the guidelines calculate the total number of vehicles that can be allowed into the park at any time. The model first calculates the total number of vehicles that can stand on the entire road length of the tourism zone @ two vehicles per km, multiplied by a rotation factor, calling it physical carrying capacity (PCC). Then it reduces this number to real carrying capacity (RCC) by applying correction factors for erosion, disturbance (during breeding seasons) and maintenance closure. The RCC is reduced into effective carrying capacity by adjusting it for management capacity based on the paucity of staff. The number so arrived, i.e. RCC, is divided between morning and evening excursions.

This entire exercise seems to be an effort to reach a predetermined low capacity, rather than deciding the carrying capacity objectively. Let us look at every step of the model and examine the logic behind each.

- Total Road Length: 283 Km
- Distance required between adjacent vehicles: 500m
- Duration of each excursion: 3.5 hours
- Total duration for excursions in a day: 9 hours
- Rotation Factor (RF): 9÷3.5 = 2.57 or 2.6
- Physical Carrying Capacity (PCC): 283×2×2.6= 1471.5 or 1472

The rotation factor is an unnecessary complication. The park is neither open throughout the day nor do the visitors enter the park all day. Visitors are allowed to enter and exit the park together in the mornings and afternoons. As there usually are only two rounds, the value of the rotation factor, if it had to be used at all, should have been 2 rather than 3.5, although that would have depressed the ECC even further. In fact calculations without using the rotation factor would have made much more sense, as it would have directly given the CC for each excursion time.

- Road length prone to erosion: 90 km (moderate erosion: 50 km, heavy erosion: 40 km)
- Correction factor for erosion (CFe): 100 — (50×2+40×3) ÷ 283×100 = 22.26% or 0.22
- RCC after adjusting for erosion: 1472×0.22 = 323.84 or 324

Road lengths that are moderately and highly prone to erosion have been given a weightage of 2 and 3 for generating the correction factor. But the way the weightage is used is completely inexplicable. It would have been much more comprehensible if the model had reduced the permissible load on such roads from 2 vehicles per km to 1 per km or 1 per 2 km and then calculated the RCC.

As one can see, although only 31.8% of the road is prone to some degree of erosion, it reduces the CC of the park by 78%. Even if one completely stops traffic on erosion sensitive roads, the CC would have been reduced only by 31.8%. But the strange application of the correction factor has wiped out the CC almost entirely.

Similarly, the correction factors developed for adjusting the CC for disturbance to different species are equally bizarre. Although the sensitivity of chital, tiger and barasingha to disturbance is presumed for 2 months, 2 months and 1 month, respectively — 5 months in all — the model presumes that there will be no tourist traffic in the park for 5 months and, thus, CC is depressed by another 45% as shown below:

- Total period for which the park is open in a year: 9 months
- Sensitive period for chital, tiger and barasingha: 5 months
- Correction factor (CFw): 100 — (5÷9 ×100) = 44.4% or 0.44
- RCC after adjusting for disturbance sensitivity: 324×0.44 = 142.56 or 143

A similar correction factor has been developed for a possible two-week closure of some roads for maintenance, etc. Obviously such a closure should have no effect on the carrying capacity on days when all roads are open. But the model depresses the CC further by applying another correction factor as shown below:

- Total weeks for which the park opens in a year: 36 weeks
- Period of closure: 2 weeks
- Correction factor for closure (CFt): 100 — (2÷36×100) = 95% or 0.95
- RCC after adjusting for temporary road closure: 143×0.95 = 135.85 or 136

After making all these adjustments, the model again assumes that Kanha management can handle only 30% of this traffic because of various deficiencies like staff vacancies. Thus the effective CC is only 40.8 or 40 vehicles. This is called the Effective Permissible Carrying Capacity (ECC) in these computations. This number is divided between morning (25) and evening rounds (15). Thus the final number comes out to be less than 3% of the PCC of the park.

It is obvious that the above methodology is extremely flawed. If a particular road section is erosion prone, the logical solution would be to reduce traffic on that road, rather than reducing the intake for the entire park. Reducing the traffic load on non-vulnerable road sections to help vulnerable sections is incomprehensible. In the computations, nearly five months out of nine are treated as sensitive when tigers, barasingha or spotted deer supposedly breed or rut and, therefore, deserve a reduction in disturbance. As a matter of fact, most animals do not care about disturbance or privacy in such matters, and tigers and spotted deer really have no definite breeding season, particularly in central India. But presuming these assumptions are correct, reducing the numbers in other months too is simply whimsical.

In fact the way the correction or reduction factors are used even in the original paper by Ceballos-Lascurain, on which the NTCA model is based, is quite bizarre and incomprehensible, and NTCA has accepted these calculations blindly. One can understand that the total intake should be reduced depending upon the limitations of the site, such as vulnerability to erosion, sensitive seasons for animal breeding, etc. One can also accept that some of these reductions will have to be rather empirical as there is no way one can exactly calculate, say, how much disturbance the animals can tolerate without harm during their breeding season. One can also grant, for reasons of convenience, that rather than using these limitations to regulate traffic in a particular area or season, one can consider reducing the total capacity for the entire park or year, although it is quite arbitrary. But rather than simply adding these correction factors to arrive at the final number, the model uses a convoluted route to arrive at the final number. The model first calculates the percentage of the road or months that need to be closed to tourism traffic. Then the percentage is reversed by deducting it out of 100 and then all the reversed factors are multiplied with the calculated PCC. A much simpler approach would have been to decide, based on the best empirical judgment of local authorities, by what percentage the usage of a road in a particular season should be reduced to preserve the quality of experience, the integrity of the site and interest of wildlife, and then reduce the PCC accordingly. These calculations can then be refined on the basis of actual experience periodically. For example, if an area seems too crowded even at the calculated traffic density or a road needs too much maintenance, traffic on such sections can be further reduced.

In fact calculating carrying capacity mechanically or mathematically is absolute nonsense where the real issues are unquantifiable commodities, such as aesthetic value of the site, the quality of visitor experience, and the concern about the safety and integrity of the resource being visited. Lower numbers of visitors can improve all these aspects but will also lower the benefits which are inherent in allowing tourism in PAs. Perhaps the best experience in wilderness is when you or your group are alone in the entire park or on a trail, and there will be no impact on the park if there are no visitors, However, as we have to provide an opportunity to as large a number of people as we reasonably can, reasonable compromises have to be made with regard to the experience of the visitors as well as the potential impact on the site, which can also be managed to some extent. A mathematical formula can give us a number that can be physically *packed* into a given space, but it cannot calibrate the quality of experience or the impact on site. These have to be determined by the local authorities and other stakeholders, depending upon what kind of experience they want to offer and how much impact on the resources is manageable on a site-specific basis.

Of course, the concerns used in the NTCA's model computations, namely, the risk of erosion, sensitivity of breeding seasons and breeding sites, and regulatory capacity of the local management, etc. are genuine, but the way these considerations have been incorporated in the computations — to deliberately depress the numbers — is irrational to say the least. Although some kind of mathematics can be used to arrive at a crude carrying capacity for a site or an area, it must be tempered with fine value judgment by the local management in consultation with other stakeholders.

Carrying capacity limits for safari vehicles were imposed in four important parks of MP in January 2008. A comparison of the calculations made by us, using the numbers given i the NTCA model brings out the above absurdity clearly.

We computed the carrying capacity of these tiger reserves using the same logic as advised by NTCA but with a bit more rational application of the correction factors. The following norms and correction factors were used in the computations:

a. Average distance between two vehicles: 500 metres, as used in the NTCA model;

b. Permissible traffic on moderately erosion prone roads: 50% of normal;

c. Permissible traffic on highly erosion prone roads: 33% of normal;

d. Permissible traffic in sensitive habitats (e.g., breeding areas of barasingha): 50% of normal; and

e. The tourism zone was divided into sub-zones for the sake of micromanagement, and carrying capacity for each sub-zone was calculated separately.

The calculations made by us for Kanha Tiger Reserve, using the modified NTCA model, are given on the next page.

Table:4 Carrying Capacity for the Entry of Tourist Vehicles in

Kanha National Park as Calculated by MP Forest Department

Zone	Total Road Length in km (L)	Roads Prone to Moderate Erosion in km (L1)	Roads Prone to Heavy Erosion in km (L2)	Roads in the Sensitive Habitats in km (L3)	PCC: @2/km (L×2)	(CFe1): Less for Moderate Erosion (50% for L1)	(CFe2): Less for Heavy Erosion (66% for L2)	(CFw): Less for Sensitive Habitats (50% for L3)	RCC (PCC-CFe1-CFe2-CFw)	CFm: Reduction Factor for Low Managerial Capacity	ECC (RCC X RFm)
Kanha	165	26	20	90	330	26	30	90	184	40%	73.6 or 70
Mukki	125	20	16	75	250	20	24	75	131	40%	52.4 or 50
Sarhi	90	18	14	52	180	18	21	52	9	40%	35.6 or 30
Total	370	64	50	217	760	64	75	217	404	40%	150

The experience since the application of the carrying capacity (150 vehicles) in the park since January 2008 shows that this number is a bit higher for some areas and needed some rationalization, which was being done by the field officers as they deemed fit. As far as the NTCA's prescription is concerned, the revised calculations (40 vehicles) based on current road length and zonation would have been a gross underutilization of the resources with very limited benefits accruing to the park and the communities. However, after the new guidelines came into effect, the new administrators of the forest department took a more pragmatic approach and have brought the number down to exactly half of the earlier number, arguing, though erroneously, that the calculated number (150) should have been divided between the morning and evening rounds. Although this argument is erroneous, because we had not used the rotation factor in the calculations at all, the new arrangement seems to have bought them peace with the NTCA, despite the fact that the number is still far above the NTCA's estimation. The forest department could not have enlarged the tourism zone to lighten the burden of some overused patches, as the NTCA has capped the size of the tourism zone at the current level. It is a small matter, though, that thousands of poor people have lost their jobs and some businesses may have gone bankrupt in the process!

The guidelines reach the height of absurdity when they say that "Management of habitat to *inflate* animal abundance for tourism purposes shall not be practiced within the core or critical habitat." Perhaps the authors wanted to prohibit creating water holes, salt licks, viewing lanes, etc. primarily to create better viewing opportunities for visitors, but ended up saying something absolutely ridiculous. This is what you call, again, throwing the baby out with the bathwater. Increasing animal abundance in the parks, tourism zone or not, is the primary job of the manager. As the punishment for the violation of these guidelines is jail, every good manager is at risk of ending up there because the increase in wildlife abundance often happens in the tourism zones first.

Obviously, the NTCA has been pursuing this line in the name of reducing impact on wildlife and its habitats. Although this so-called impact of tourism on wildlife is not visible anywhere in the country, except minor aberrations here and there, some impact may, in fact, be a small price to pay for the benefits that tourism confers on the conservation agencies and the local and national economies as a whole. A country struggling to feed and house more than a billion people, most of them utterly poor, has to eke out whatever benefits it can from its natural resources. If that means some unavoidable, harmless inconvenience to animals, the animals will still be the gainers.

Not many people in the country seem to be aware of the potential of these guidelines for damaging the conservation scene in the country. This is a mistake which will have countrywide impact and will kill all creativity and innovation in conservation, as no officer would like to risk going to jail by violating these guidelines. These guidelines also highlight the dangers of the proclivity of central agencies to issue advisories to the states on operational matters. In a federal structure, the states should be encouraged to innovate according to their own vision and needs rather than forcing them to follow a roadmap created by far away strangers.

Forest (Conservation) Act 1980 and Ecotourism

A concern has been bothering many foresters in India as to whether or not ecotourism is "a non-forest purpose" in the context of the Forest (Conservation) Act, 1980 (FCA). As forest officers are competent to allow people to enter the forests under IFA as well as WLPA, the bare act of letting visitors into the forest should not be a problem. However, development of infrastructure for facilitating ecotourism in forests does seem to attract FCA, at least prima facie. Therefore, a brief discussion on this issue may not be out of place here.

The Forest (Conservation) Act 1980 provides, among other things, that prior permission of GoI is required before allowing the use of any forest land for any "non-forest purpose" or before "assigning" a forest land to any entity not controlled by the government.

The expression "non-forest purpose" is defined in the Act as "breaking up or clearing of any forest land" for "any purpose other than reafforestation" but does not include "any work relating or ancillary to conservation, development and management of forests and wildlife, namely, the establishment of check posts, fire lines, wireless communications and construction of fencing, bridges and culverts, dams, waterholes and trench marks, boundary marks, pipelines or other like purposes".

States cannot "assign" any forest land, by way of lease or otherwise, to any private entity without the prior permission of GoI. For "assigning", there are no exceptions given in the Act, unlike the "non-forest use". However, the states have been violating both the cardinal provisions from the beginning. The state forest departments regularly do several things on the forest land which are not included in the list of exceptions, like building forest rest houses, staff quarters, godowns, depots, extraction paths, etc. and also "assign" forest lands to various entities, without the permission of the GoI. The department has been "assigning" the forest lands to various kinds of contractors, like timber haulage contractors, *tendu* leaf contractors and cooperative societies. In fact, the states have "assigned" most of their forests to joint forest management committees (JFMCs).

MP has, additionally, assigned the entire forest area to the primary cooperative societies for the collection of *tendu* leaf and other minor forest products. Quite justifiably, though, no questions have ever been raised as to whether these activities were "non-forest purpose" or whether the kind of "assigning" being done was within the law or not, because all these actions were meant to be a part of the process of forest management, although the law does not allow "assigning" of forest land even for this purpose. In fact, because the mandate of the forest department is to conserve and manage the forests, whatever the department does is considered to be in pursuit of this mandate only. On the same lines, states have also been allowing wildlife tourism in the protected areas for nearly half a century. Of late, the states have started trying to spread the footprint of ecotourism even outside wildlife sanctuaries in view of the global experience in using ecotourism as a tool for conservation of forests and wildlife. Under the circumstances, ecotourism, like so many other activities mentioned above, should have been naturally treated as something being "ancillary to conservation, development and management of forests and wildlife".

However, in a communication to the Haryana forest department, the GoI has held that "……. ecotourism is not a forestry activity ……. " which means prior permission of GoI is required before letting people enjoy the natural beauty of our forests. This letter, though meant only for Haryana in the context of a specific project for which they had sought GoI permission, has found its way into the hands of every forester, and many of them are now scared of even uttering the word ecotourism. It makes even the traditional wildlife tourism look illegal under FCA, although, strangely, the controversy about wildlife tourism is being discussed only in the context of the WLPA. So much so that the Auditor General has branded everything done by the MP Ecotourism Development Board since its inception in 2005 as illegal in the light of this letter and has advised the Board to seek GoI permission for everything they have done so far. PCCF of MP requested the GoI to calibrate the GoI stand on the issue, rather than banning it completely, as ecotourism is not a single activity or action, but was contemptuously snubbed by the DGF. We are now in a peculiar situation where the NTCA is trying to stop tourism within PAs in the name of the WLPA and the ministry is trying to stop it outside PAs in the name of FCA. If this situation persists, Indians will have to go abroad to see any wildlife or natural beauty.

As ecotourism unequivocally enhances the protection of forests and wildlife, there should be no doubt about its clubbing with the exceptions given in the Act under the category "other like purposes", even if it involves limited clearance of forest lands. Not only should people be encouraged to enter forests for ecotourism, some basic infrastructure, such as toilets, camping sites, shades, hides, *machaans,* etc. can also be constructed like so many other things we do in the forests to strengthen conservation, without attracting the provisions of the FCA. Similarly, assigning forest areas to private or joint venture entities for running ecotourism activities (not developing residential complexes) should not attract the provisions of the FCA, as it is no different from the kind of assigning the states are already doing. Of course, there will be some risk of people going too far in the name of *basic* infrastructure, but such cases can be made rare exceptions if a proper climate is created, impressing on authorities what is or is not ecotourism. In any case, the fear of exceptions cannot be the reason for not making a rule.

Conclusion

Ecotourism or wildlife tourism has always been part of human life; earlier it was in the form of hunting and now it is more in the form of watching and photographing natural beauty and wildlife. Nearly every document on conservation of natural resources, in India and abroad, talks about the relevance of ecotourism. As mentioned before, most of the famous landscapes have been preserved, along with their constituent flora and fauna, primarily because they were reserved for tourism or recreation in time. The National Forest Commission even calls it the "new mantra" for conservation. As such, talking about banning ecotourism anywhere, or reducing it to insignificant levels, sounds quite incongruous. If the laws made before the realization of the significance of ecotourism in conservation and poverty alleviation need to be fine-tuned, it should be done forthwith.

The world over, efforts are being made to position ecotourism primarily as pro-poor tourism (PPT). Although every economic activity is a pro-poor activity because the basic services and goods are ultimately provided by the unskilled and poor workers, tourism by its very nature is a particularly pro-poor industry because the scope for creating jobs for the unskilled workers in the remote areas, as well as along the travel route, is much higher than in other businesses. Incidentally, the effect of ecotourism on poverty alleviation is quite limited as of now because of leakages (Bookbinder *et al.* 1998, B.C. Sinha *et al.* 2013), but its potential is huge. Fortunately, the leakages are much lower in India than in other countries as nearly all the tourism businesses are owned by Indians and nearly all the workers are Indian (Ashley *et al.* 2000). Whatever leakage happens, it happens only within the country, which again creates jobs within the country only. However, efforts have to be continuously made so that most of the revenue generated by tourism businesses is spent close to the destinations and that the locals and tribals are enabled to benefit from tourism jobs and businesses to the maximum. Discussions about how much and what kind of tourism should be allowed, on a site specific basis, should be encouraged, and efforts to maximize the benefits to conservation and local communities should be the core of these discussions. India has just been discovered by the international travellers, and the Indians themselves have just acquired some affluence to allow them to think a bit beyond concerns of just making a living. Therefore, the real impact of ecotourism on the Indian economy and ecology is yet to unfold. Any discourse about scotching or stifling ecotourism shall amount to abandoning this tool for removing rural poverty, especially in remote areas, even before testing its efficacy.

5

Hunting for Conservation

The word "hunting" basically means the killing of wild animals, although there are several cognate variants of the expression. "Sport-hunting" or "recreational hunting" means the act of seeking out, pursuing and killing wild animals for the purpose of recreation; "trophy hunting" means sport-hunting of a particularly large animal for procuring a trophy, such as head, skin, tusks, etc. for display; "tourist hunting" stands for hunting by tourists, as against the locals; "conservation hunting" represents a concept in which sport hunting aims to reduce overexploitation of wildlife, caused by subsistence hunting and poaching by generating economic benefits for local people; and "biltong hunting", in South Africa, means hunting for the purpose of preparing dried meat called biltong. In this chapter, all these variants of sport-hunting have been used interchangeably, with only minor variations in meaning, depending upon the context.

In the previous chapters, we have discussed how human beings have always hunted wild animals, either for making their surroundings safer or for the goodies that the dead animals produce, or just for recreation. For the same reasons, hunting of wild animals is still prevalent, illegally. In view of the sharp decline in the numbers and spread of wildlife in the country, we have to find a way to reduce the pressure of hunting to bring exploitation within sustainable limits. We have seen that a complete ban on hunting has not produced the desired results as enforcing such a ban is virtually impossible. Most countries have a system of recreational hunting in which limited hunting by wealthy tourists produces significantly higher economic benefits for the local people in a way which creates a disincentive against mass hunting by the locals themselves. Wildlife tourism was perhaps the greatest invention of modern man as a conservation tool as it creates the justification as well as the resources required for conservation. Although viewing or photographic tourism itself can be a very strong incentive for local people to not overhunt wild animals, champions of sport-hunting believe that limited sport-hunting can increase the benefits of tourism to conservation significantly.

Why Sport-Hunting

The killing or capturing of wild animals is done by people in India — illegally of course — for all the usual reasons, namely:

1. Food for self-consumption or for trade
2. Non-food products, such as skins, bones, trophies, etc. for trade
3. To prevent or minimise losses caused by wild animals
4. Recreation or entertainment (sport-hunting)

Killing for food or other products, and for protecting crops, is primarily done by the poor people living in the forests, or by nomadic traditional hunting communities, such as *pardhis, bahelias, bawarias, mogias,* etc. Some better-off people consider wild meat as a luxury and status symbol. As the activity is illegal, people try whatever methods get them quick and cheap results. Therefore, most of the killing is done by snaring, trapping, poisoning and even electrocuting animals. In this category of hunting, age, sex and size of the killed animal is generally irrelevant. Every killer would like to get the biggest animals, but because the methods used are non-discriminating, and because any animal is better than no animal, the killing is totally indiscriminate. These methods often result in the death of untargeted species. More leopards die in the snares placed for pigs and deer around crop fields than due to targeted poaching. Although commercially important booty obtained through such activities may produce substantial incomes for the intermediaries and smuggling kingpins in the illegal market, the poor people who actually do the killing are paid very little. Their incomes generally are limited to the value of meat eaten or sold in the local market Off and on, they may get substantial sums for producing something like tiger skins and bones for smuggling, but such opportunities are few and far between.

Hunting wild animals for entertainment has been an age old passion for man. That is why the activity is called "sport-hunting" while the animals are called "game". In sport-hunting the animals are pursued and killed more for testing one's own endurance, patience and martial skills and less for meat and other products. However, the trophy, comprising the skin, head, rack (antlers) or horns that can be displayed, is also an important motive for hunting the animal. In India, the rich and the powerful indulge in illegal hunting of wild animals for recreation as well as for venison. In most countries where sport-hunting is legal, the hunter takes home only the trophy and a little meat, while the bulk of the meat is either donated to poor people (e.g., USA) or is surrendered to authorities or communities (e.g., South Africa) who dispose it off as per their own procedures. The sportsmen (hunters) spend large sums of money on hunting licenses, trophy fees, boarding, travel, accessories, etc. just for the experience of ambushing and stalking an animal. *Times of India* reported in August 2006 that China auctioned a yak hunt for 40,000 dollars. In Pakistan, the trophy fee for Suleiman *markhor* was $ 50,000 as far back as the year 2000. An old white rhino was sold in Botswana for 170,000 pounds, while license fees for two lions were reported to be close to $131,975 and $145,000. An extreme example of the hunting craze was reported in The Hunting Report Newsletter (at www.huntingreport.com) when a single Canadian bighorn sheep hunt was auctioned for 405,000 Canadian dollars in the Cadoman area, bordering Jasper National Park in 2004. And the hunter, one Sherwin Scott, could not bag the animal within the allotted 17-day hunt, after having paid all the fees.

Kwanare Game Reserve in Mpumalanga sold a male cape buffalo for 6 million Rands to Shambala Game Reserve in Limpopo; quality female buffalos are often sold for R400,000 to R600,000 ($29476 - 44215) each (Huntnetwork, June 2010).

As sport-hunting can generate far higher revenues per animal than just its meat value, it can generate far higher benefits for conservation and communities if these benefits are properly channelized than allowing everyone to hunt for food and other purposes.

Pro-Hunting and Anti-Hunting Lobbies

As expected, sport-hunting is a controversial subject, with vociferous lobbies on both sides of the divide. While the hunters think it is their money and advocacy which is saving the wildlife of the world, their opponents, mainly the animal rights lobbies, say that hunting is a cruel practice that does more harm to wild populations than any perceived good. Some of these arguments have been briefly mentioned in the previous pages, but it will be useful to put them all together again and compare their logic for better understanding.

Justification for Sport-Hunting:

1.   The Rocky Mountain Elk Foundation on its websi te (http://www.rmef.org/Conservation/HuntingIsC onservation/25ReasonsWhyHuntingIsConservat ion.aspx) lists the following 25 reasons why "hunting is conservation":

a)   In 1907, only 41,000 elk remained in North America. Thanks to the money and hard work invested by hunters to restore and conserve their habitat, today there are more than 1 million.

b) In 1900, only 500,000 whitetails remained. Thanks to conservation work spearheaded by hunters, today there are more than 32 million.

c) In 1900, only 100,000 wild turkeys remained. Thanks to hunters, today there are over 7 million.

d) In 1901, few ducks remained. Thanks to hunters" efforts to restore and conserve wetlands, today there are more than 44 million.

e) In 1950, only 12,000 pronghorn remained. Thanks to hunters, today there are more than 1.1 million.

f) Habitat, research and wildlife law enforcement work, all paid for by hunters, help countless non-hunted species.

g) Through state licenses and fees, hunters pay $796 million a year for conservation programs.

h) Through donations to groups like RMEF, hunters add $440 million a year to conservation efforts.

i) In 1937, hunters actually requested an 11% tax on guns, ammo, bows and arrows to help fund conservation. That tax has, so far, raised more than $7.2 billion for wildlife conservation.

j) An 11% tax on guns, ammo, bows and arrows generates $371 million a year for conservation.

k) Altogether, hunters pay more than $1.6 billion a year for conservation programs. No one gives more!

l) Three out of four Americans approve of hunting, partly because hunters are America's greatest positive force for conservation.

m)   As taxpayers, hunters also fund the U.S. Fish and Wildlife Service, U.S. Forest Service, etc.

n)   Hunting funds conservation AND the economy, generating $38 billion a year in retail spending.

o)   Hunting supports 680,000 jobs, from game wardens to waitresses, biologists to motel clerks.

p)   Hunters are the fuel behind RMEF and its 6.3 million-plus acres of habitat conservation. More than 95 percent of our 196,000 members are passionate hunters.

q)   A wildlife management tool, hunting helps balance wildlife populations with what the land can support, limits crop damage and curtails disease outbreaks.

r)   Hunters help manage growing numbers of predators such as cougars, bears, coyotes and wolves. Our government spends millions to control predators and varmints while hunters have proven more than willing to pay for that opportunity.

s)   Hunting has major value for highway safety. For every deer hit by a motorist, hunters take six.

t)   Deer collisions kill 200 motorists and cost $10 billion a year. Imagine costs without hunting!

u)   Hunters provide for conservation — and for their families. Hunting is a healthy way to connect with nature and eat the world's most organic, lean, free-range meat.

v)   Hunter numbers are down, while hunter spending for conservation is up. Unequalled devotion!

w)   Avid hunter Theodore Roosevelt created our national forests and grasslands and forever protected 230 million acres for wildlife and the public to use and enjoy.

x)   With funding from hunters, RMEF helped restore wild elk herds in six states and provinces.

y)   As society loses its ties to wildlife and conservation, the bonds with nature formed by hunting are the greatest hope for creating the next generation of true conservationists.

2.   Several countries in Africa, such as Tanzania, Uganda, Zambia, Zimbabwe, Cameroon, Burkina Faso, Botswana, Namibia, etc. are implementing community-based wildlife management programmes, adjacent to well-known protected areas, in which trophy hunting is a major component. Variously called as Community Conservancies, Game Management Areas (GMA) or Wildlife Management Areas (WMAs), these areas act as buffer zones and wildlife corridors between protected areas, and thus provide the much needed incremental space for migratory animals and animals with large home ranges. These programmes are becoming major tools for rural development, employment generation and conservation of natural resources in Africa. The principal source of income to these communities is trophy hunting[3].

3.   "Project Noah is an educational and training program run in collaboration with the international hunting fraternity. This program has

as its main goal the education and training of rural youth from wildlife rich areas throughout Sub-Saharan Africa in the sustainable utilization and conservation of wildlife and associated habitats. It also exposes them to the value of wildlife and how it can serve as a powerful economic and rural development tool. This training takes place at the Department of Nature Conservation, Tshwane University of Technology (TUT), South Africa. Through the education and training of students and establishing them back in their countries of origin, it is believed that the following objectives are being achieved (among many others):

a. Creating a core of scientific expertise where students will become the future community wildlife managers, safari operators, government decision makers, or conservation NGO coordinators;

b. Ensuring that the utilization (hunting) of wildlife in Africa remains (becomes) a viable option of income generation, thereby ensuring that future generations of sport hunters can continue to practice their sport.

Upon completion of their training, the idea is to plant Noah graduates back into their communities where they can integrate their new found knowledge into traditional management systems in finding an African solution to conservation that integrates rural Africans into a multiple-resource use conservation model, seen as an important component of the way forward.

To date over 50 students from all of the major hunting countries in Africa have been provided with scholarships supported by the international sport-hunting fraternity, including Shikar Safari Club, Dallas Safari Club and Safari Club International. The success of this program can be determined from the fact that the majority of these students have returned to their countries and/or communities and are actively using their new found skills and insight into the wildlife trade to further conservation and community development." (DeGeorges and Reilly 2009).

4.   The CAMPFIRE (Communal Areas Management Programme for Indigenous Resources) programme of Zimbabwe, which is the forerunner of many community-based conservation programmes across the globe, generates 90% of its income from trophy hunting. Poaching had gone down significantly, although things are not as rosy as before, since the political turmoil and land reforms introduced a few years ago. The project has created thousands of jobs and built many schools, clinics and other community structures (Global Eye-focus on Sustainable Development, case study: CAMPFIRE, Zimbabwe: www.globaleye.org.uk).

5.   The Community Based Natural Resource Management (CBNRM) programme in Namibia, under which community conservancies have been established around protected areas, is recognised as a shining example of sport-hunting

benefitting wildlife as well as poor rural communities. According to the profile of a conservancy called the Nyae Nyae Conservancy (Living with wildlife: the story of Nyae Nyae Conservancy – www.nacso.org.na), 50% of the approximately $3,000,000 household income accruing to the members of the conservancy came from trophy hunting in 2010, while the wildlife populations in the conservancy continue to grow. The total population of game animals in the conservancy grew from just 1504 in 1998 to 5274 in 2003 (including 2157 introductions) (Weaver and Skyer 2003).

6.   In an authentic analysis of the *markhor* (Capra *falconeri*) conservation programmes in the North West Frontier Province (NWFP) and North areas of Pakistan over an 18 year period up to 2006, Sajid Ali (2008) writes that, "Pakistan has led the world in introducing the concept of community-based trophy hunting programs (CTHP) for the conservation of biodiversity in high alpine ecosystems. Limited trophy hunting has been practiced in Pakistan since the 1980s in Balochistan, NWFP, and Northern Areas as a management tool for the conservation of Suleiman *markhor*, Afghan *urial* (Ovis *vignei blandfordi*), Punjab *urial* (Ovis vignei punjabiensis), Sindh *ibex* (*Caprahircus blythi*), flare-horned *markhor*, and Himalayan ibex (Capra *ibex sibirica*). Benefits (fees) from the hunts were used for the conservation and protection of the species. In 1983, the NWFP

Wildlife Department (WD) started the Chitral Conservation Hunting Program (CTHHP), a trophy hunting program for *markhor*. This was not a community based conservation (CBC) program because all proceeds went to the government. In 1993, the NWFP WD (wildlife department) embarked upon a program of community participation in wildlife conservation. Communities were organized and two areas (Gehrait and Tooshi Shasha) were declared as community managed conservation areas (CMCAs), called conservancies, in Chitral with the consent of the local communities. A trophy hunting policy was approved which stated that 75% of the trophy hunting fee would go to communities. Subsequently, the Government of Pakistan (GoP) submitted a proposal to CITES for allocation of an annual trophy hunting quota for *markhor* to act as an incentive for the communities to conserve *markhor*. CITES (1997) approved an annual *markhor* trophy hunting quota of six animals for Pakistan subject to the condition that trophy hunting would be allowed only in CMCAs. Due to the success of the CTHP, CITES (2002) increased the trophy hunting quota for Pakistan from 6 to 12 for CMCAs to further encourage communities" involvement in the conservation of *markhor*. The records of NWFP wildlife department show that 28 hunting permits for *markhor* have been issued in CMCAs from 1998 to 2007 and 75-80% of the permit fee has been deposited in the village conservation funds (VCF) as the communities' share."

Out of a total earning of $ 1,057,500, three conservancies — namely, Tooshi Shasha Conservancy (TSC) in District Chitral, Gehrait Goleen Conservancy in District Chitral and Kaigah Nullah Conservancy in District Kohistan — received a sum of $ 843,300 during this period. The trophy fees went up from $ 18,000 per animal in 1998-99 to $ 57,100 in 2006-07. The communities used these funds for building their social infrastructure, apart from paying the "village wildlife watchers". Poaching has gone down considerably as the communities have to pledge to stop hunting as a condition of constituting a conservancy. As a result, the wildlife populations in all the conservancies have grown as fast as in the strictly protected national parks of the area. For example, "The estimated rate of increase in the *markhor* population in Chitral Gol National Park (CGNP) was 7.7% over the 18 years of this study. The population growth rate was estimated to be 2.5% over 10 years (1989-1998) before CTHP was launched in 1998 in CBC areas, while the growth rate was 12.8% during 9 years afterwards (1998-2006)...the *markhor* population growth rate in TSC was estimated 7.9% per year over 18 year." The total population of *markhor* in CGNP (77.5 sq km) grew from 154 in 1990 to 612 in 2006, while the population in TSC (200 sq km) grew from 137 to 545 during the same period. "*Comparison of growth rates (total population, male population, male/female ratio) during pre and post period of CTHP showed higher growth rates during the trophy hunting program."*

"The communities supported and became involved in conservation and protection of *markhor* and other wildlife species in their areas .... As a result, poaching was controlled to a large extent in almost all communities ... In fact, the Government has to expend a lot of resources for the conservation of *markhor* through watch and ward activities. However, communities-based wildlife management is cost effective for the Government."

Recognizing the importance of CTHP in conservation, many international donor and conservation organizations such as UNDP, IUCN, WWF, EU, etc. have been continuously supporting these programmes with funds and technical knowhow, through projects like the Himalayan Jungle Project (HJP) and Maintaining Biodiversity in Pakistan with Rural Development Pre-Investment Feasibility (PRIF) Phase, followed by the Mountain Areas Conservation Project (MACP).

"Trophy hunting is often advantageous both ecologically and economically, because it requires little infrastructure, draws small crowds, produces less litter than ecotourism, and only a small fraction of the population, i.e. old males having aesthetic value, are harvested. This activity often generates more revenue than ecotourism from a small number of trophy hunters .... hunters willingly pay relatively more money for the privilege of hunting an unusual trophy animal. Importantly, the revenue so generated can be used for conservation of biodiversity through involvement of local communities. Trophy hunting has great potential and serves as an important source of incentives for local people especially in areas where the tourism industry cannot be developed due to political instability... Trophy hunting has been integrated into many conservation programs and projects as a conservation tool for sustainability of wildlife resources and improved socio-economic conditions of the communities ...... This approach can be adopted for the conservation of wildlife outside of national parks and areas which lack alternative wildlife-based land uses such as photographic ecotourism... Likewise, trophy hunting can be used as a tool for the conservation of endangered species even when excessive exploitation might be the original cause of the conservation problem ..... The benefits of properly managed and monitored trophy hunting outweigh any of its disadvantages. Moreover, the individuals selected for trophy hunting are usually older males, some of which have little future role in breeding activity ..... Therefore, removal of these males is unlikely to affect the reproductive capacity of the population, should have a minimal effect on *markhor* genetics, and have a

negligible impact on overall population size."
(Note: I have removed all the (numerous)
references from the above text to make for easy
reading).

7.   Torghar is another tribal area in the Balochistan
province of Pakistan where impressive success
has been achieved in conservation and
community development through a trophy
hunting programme, involving *markhor* and
Afgan *urial*. Due to uncontrolled hunting,
accelerated by the easy availability of cheap
automatic weapons from the war in Afghanistan,
most wild animals were wiped out in the Torghar
Hills by the mid nineteen eighties, and only very
small populations of *markhor* and *urial* were
surviving. In an attempt to reverse the rapid
decline of population numbers, local tribal
leaders and tribesmen agreed on an
area/species-wide hunting ban and in 1984, with
technical assistance from the US Fish and
Wildlife Service, established the Torghar
Conservation Programme (TCP). In April 1994,
the TCP became an NGO called The Society for
Torghar Environmental Protection (STEP). In
1985, Dr. Richard Mitchell of the USFWS spent a
week in Torghar assessing *markhor* and *urial*
population dynamics. Based on observations and
interviews with the local people, he estimated
that the *markhor* population was less than 100
and that the *urial* population stood at 200+. On
the basis of the survey, the hunting of 1-2 *urial*
was considered feasible. Since then trophy

hunting has been going on in the area and local people have been employed as game guards whose number has grown to 68 from the initial 7. Although 18-20 rams can be annually harvested without affecting the population or its growth rate in any way, no more than 4 animals are hunted annually. Poaching by the locals and outsiders has been completely controlled. Local people have reduced their livestock herds to "drought" levels in order to reduce competition with wildlife. In November 1994, Dr. Mitchel conducted a scientific census, which indicated that the area within STEP contained a population of around 700+ *markhor* and 1200+ *urial*. Estimates of the 1999 survey by Mike Frisina show 1684+ *markhor* and 1752+ *urial*. After deducting the operating costs, the government takes 25% of the income from trophy hunting fees whilst 75% is forwarded to community organizations. The communities have also been receiving assistance from UNDP/GEF, the Houbara Foundation and WWF, etc. These incomes have been used to build community assets like drinking water facilities, irrigation facilities, health camps, etc.

It is important to note that *markhor* is included in schedule III of the Balochistan Wildlife Protection Act, 1974, and its hunting can be allowed only in exceptional situations. Similarly, the species is in Appendix I of the CITES and its commercial export/ import is forbidden. Despite such severe restrictions, the provincial and national governments as well as CITES have made an exception by allowing trophy hunting and export of *markhor* trophies because the program is seen as helping conservation as well as communities (Source: Ahmed Javed *et al.* 2001; Woodford *et al.* undated).

8.   In an exhaustive study aptly entitled as "Potential Cost of Losing Hunting and Trapping as Wildlife Management Methods", the International Association of Fish and Wildlife Agencies (2005) come up with the following conclusions for the USA:

- Economy will lose money spent by hunters: e.g., $847 mn in license fee/taxes, $5.2 bn in hotel/food and travel expenses.

- Losses caused by wildlife: e.g., road accidents $1 bn, damage to households $633 mn, crop and livestock losses $944 mn, losses to timber industry $750 mn. These losses will increase 221% per annum if wildlife is not hunted.

- Potential loss to timber industry if wildlife populations are not managed will be $8.3 bn.

- Auto accidents are a major consequence of having wildlife. It is estimated that the current estimate of 729,000 accidents per year shall grow by 218% and will result in 50,000 more human injuries and $3.8 bn in terms of additional auto repairs.

- Increase in wildlife populations shall result in an increase in the incidence of rabies, which will require an additional sum of $1.45 bn per annum to control.

- Although translocation and culling through sharp shooters is not a viable option for many other reasons, the cost ($ 9.5 bn) itself will make these solutions impractical.

- Accidents caused by wild animals will result in aircraft damages worth nearly $528 mn per annum.

- The total cost of not hunting wild animals in America is estimated to be **$70.8 bn per annum.**

9.   In a peer-reviewed report entitled "Shooting Sports – findings of an economic and environmental survey", Public and Corporate Economic Consultants (PACEC), 2006, reported that 480,000 shooters in the UK created 70,000 full time jobs and spent nearly £2 bn in rural areas. The value of the sport to the economy was estimated to be £1.6 bn in terms of employment and profits. An area of £2 million ha is being managed for conservation, on which the shoot providers spent 250 million per annum. In addition, the shooters spent 2.7 million work days on conservation work, which is equivalent to 12,000 full time jobs. More than half the shooting time of 970,000 days per annum is spent on shooting the species considered pests, such as pigeons and rabbits. In the absence of shooting, the 61,000 shooting providers shall incur an annual cost of £9800 each on pest control. The land actually managed by shooting providers for conservation (2 million ha) dwarfs the 87,900 ha under the National Nature

Reserve and the 87,000 ha managed by Wildlife Trusts. Shooting providers spent £8 mn on planting trees in 2004. The land managed for shooting supports many non-game species. Shooting provides income to rural youth and hotels in winter and autumn when other incomes are absent.

10. The US Fish and Wildlife Service (US FWS), in collaboration with the US Census Bureau, has been publishing a report called "A National Survey of Fishing, Hunting and Wildlife-Associated Recreation" every five years since 1955. The 2011 report was released in February 2014. The highlights of the 2011 report are as follows:

"37.4 million sportsmen, i.e. anglers and hunters, spent $89.8 bn over 836 mn days of recreational fishing and hunting in 2011, while 71.8 mn wildlife watchers also spent $54.9 bn during the same year. The number of total recreationists grew from 87.4 mn to 90.1 mn persons between 2006 and 2011, but most of this increase was in the category of sportsmen, going from 33.9 mn to 37.39 mn while the number of wildlife watchers grew only marginally, from 71.1 mn to 71.7 mn. Although the wildlife watchers still outnumber sportsmen significantly, but, interestingly, only 22.4 mn wildlife watchers went beyond one km from their residences in 2011 which is even lower than the number in 2006, standing at 22.9 mn."

11. Munn et al (2010) analysed the 2006 survey report (A National Survey of Fishing, Hunting and Wildlife-Associated Recreation) of the USFWS, (http://www.census.gov/prod/2008pubs/fhw0 6-nat.pdf) mentioned above, for its economic impact in the South-eastern region of the US, which generated about 35% of the total recreational expenditures in the country. According to them, out of a total expenditure of $32.8 bn, $21.12 bn came out of the pockets of hunters and anglers and out of 397,105 jobs created by the wildlife-associated recreation activity, 228,724 were created by sportsmen. The activity created an overall economic impact equivalent to $53.88 bn, out of which $32.48 bn was due to the expenditures incurred by sportsmen. Total economic output due to this activity was 0.68% of the gross output of the region, while the employment generation was 0.69% of the gross employment generation by the region's economy.

12. During the late 19th century and much of the 20th century, efforts to protect bio-diversity in Africa emphasized the designation of protected areas. The emphasis on protected areas began to shift during the 1970s with the recognition that islands of protection are inadequate for maintaining spatially heterogeneous biodiversity. Many wildlife species exhibit extensive and unpredictable movements across the landscape. Biological challenges are also created by the fact that many species require

large home ranges and form metapopulations. The Greater Limpopo Transfrontier Conservation area (GLTFCA) encompassing wild lands in South Africa, Zimbabwe and Mozambique was conceived in the context of these requirements. GLTFCA will be nearly 100,000 sq km when fully incorporated and will include fully functional protected areas, community conserved areas and private game reserves situated in this landscape in all the participating countries. Although most protected areas also have wildlife hunting programmes in Africa, the primary objective of the communal and private game reserves is the utilization of wildlife for trophy hunting or meat production. The inclusion of these entities in the conservation planning of this landscape is in recognition of the fact that the conservationists do not treat hunting of wildlife as contradictory to the principles of conservation.

A key driver of the development of vibrant wildlife industries in South Africa and Zimbabwe in the 1980s and 1990s was the legislative change that allowed private landowners to utilize and manage wildlife on their land without government permits. There are approximately 5,000 game ranches and over 4,000 mixed game and livestock ranches in South Africa, which jointly cover about 170,000 km. This area of private land supporting wildlife comprises about 14% of South Africa's land area, compared to 6.3% declared as formal conservation areas.

About 45% of the game ranches are located in the Limpopo Province, where they cumulatively covered around 36,000 km^2 in 1998, about twice the size of the Kruger National Park. Under the National Parks Act of 1976, private land located next to national parks could be designated as a "contracted national park". In actuality, private land adjacent to the Kruger National Park has not yet been granted contracted park status.

What has happened is that the national park and the five private reserves ……. namely, Sabi Sands, Klaserie, Timbavati, Balule, and Umbabat ……. situated on its western boundary have dropped the fences which divided them. In order to remove fences separating private land from the Kruger National Park, an agreement was signed by the Association of Private Nature Reserves (APNR) with South African National Parks to manage wildlife within the reserves according to the master plan for the Kruger National Park. Free movement of wildlife across the APNR reserves and along the west–east river systems has been made possible by fence removals within and between reserves and Kruger. In Zimbabwe, the private conservancies near the Gonarezhou National Park include Malilangwe, Hippo Valley, Chiredzi River, Save Valley, and Bubiana and Bubi River, and wildlife corridors have been proposed to link them to the Gonarezhou National Park. The Save Valley Conservancy was established when 23 ranchers replaced their fences with a single rhino-proof game fence around their combined properties. This led to the formation of one of the world's largest private nature reserves, covering 345,067 hectares (3,450 square kilometers) (Kreuter *et al.* 2010).

The most interesting part of this arrangement is that these private nature reserves, or conservancies, continue to pursue their hunting objectives while being part of the extended Kruger National Park, showing that the hunting reserves and the traditional protected areas both can have common objectives. For example, the constitution of the Klaserie Private Nature Reserve states that its objective is "to conserve a wide diversity of indigenous species and their associated habitats using sustainable utilization principles." They still shoot animals according to the total annual off-take quota specified for the reserve. Culling of overabundant species is also prescribed (Kreuter *et al.* 2010).

13.　Apart from Pakistan, Nepal also allows trophy hunting in our neighbourhood. Dhorpatan, situated in the Dhaulagiri ranges, is the only hunting reserve in the country. Permits for hunting blue sheep, Himalayan *tahr*, barking deer, etc. are issued every year. I could not find the hunting regulations applicable in Nepal on the web. However, Karki and Thapa (2011), after conducting a status survey of blue sheep and Himalayan *tahr* in the reserve, state that "The results indicated that the existing quota of blue sheep hunting can be safely continued. In case of higher demands, two more quotas can be added to Barse, Dogadi and Sundaha blocks for the next five years (2008-2012). Himalayan *tahr*s can be hunted in all the blocks. Sundaha block can sustain four while the rest of the blocks can sustain two Himalayan *tahr*s per year." No report on the impact of the programme on the social and economic conditions of the local communities could be found on the internet

No trophy hunting is allowed in Bhutan, but some reports on the internet suggest that Bhutan is contemplating tourist hunting for wild boar due to extensive crop damage http://wildb oarhunt.blogspot.com/2009/01/bhutan-wildlife-management.html).

14. Apart from trophy hunting by foreign tourists, local people also hunt wild animals for food and sport. In an evaluation report of the ADMADE CBNRM programme of Zambia, Paul Andre DeGeorges, (1992) describes the need of the local people for hunting as follows:

"Traditionally, for rural Africa wildlife has meant food. Regardless of who was interviewed during the evaluation, everyone acknowledged that in rural Zambia, the average person's perception of wildlife was something God gave the rural African to eat. Regardless of whom we talked to, the following general issues were raised:

"They have a "disease" passed on to them from their fathers; they like to hunt.

"In every family of a hunter, there will be at least one who is born with natural hunting instincts and the desire to hunt."

Do not forget the famous quote from the author Robert Ruark,

"The Horn Of The Hunter Sounds Within Us All!!"

Most Traditional Hunters feel "stabbed and sick that they can no longer pursue their calling while the wealthy white man can come from afar and legally shoot their game. In one of the Community Development Officer's reports, this has allegedly led to indiscriminate killing of wildlife by traditional hunters purely out of frustration.""

In most CBNRM projects, local residents are also allowed a quota for traditional hunting to meet their need for food and to satisfy their urge for hunting. However, they are allowed to hunt only the non-trophy game which needs to be culled for management purposes. These quotas are generally 5-6% of the estimated population but may go up to 10-15%. In some cases, even the cull quota is sold to tourists for earning more revenue for the communities (DeGeorges 1992).

15.   In South Africa, recreational hunting by local people for producing dried meat called biltong is very popular. Biltong hunting is practiced mainly over 17 million hectares of private game reserves or ranches. There are estimated to be nearly 200,000 biltong hunters in South Africa,

most of whom hunt more than once a year. According to Dr. Peet van der Merwe and Prof Melville Saayman from the University of the North West at Potchefstroom (2005), biltong hunters spend nearly 3.1 billion Rands per year on various facilities while the total contribution of hunting to the national economy is estimated to be R7.7 billion per annum. This activity is estimated to produce jobs worth more than R1.6 billion per annum while the value of the 9000 private game farms is estimated to be more than R20 billion.

Obviously, the economic value created by trophy hunting and biltong hunting is responsible for sustaining such large areas of wilderness, which provide so many ecological benefits to the world.

16. A website called "Catholic Answers" (www.catholic.com) says that "God gave man stewardship over animals, and that includes using them for just purposes. Examples of just purposes that the *Catechism of the Catholic Church* points out are food, clothing, medical and scientific experimentation, and the work and leisure of man (CCC 2417–8). Animals, properly speaking, do not have "rights" because they are not human. ……. Some use the meat and skins of the animals. Others are helping to preserve the balance of nature by using carefully regulated licensing procedures to thin out animal overpopulation. Some hunt for sport, but the sport is in the tracking, gun skills, and trophy hunting, not in causing suffering and death to

animals. All responsible hunters take care not to leave a wounded animal injured by a badly aimed shot to suffer; they make sure to track it down and end its suffering. In short, the Church does not oppose sport-hunting."

Anti-Hunting Arguments

The above examples seem to make a very strong case in support of sport-hunting as a means of conservation and development. But, as mentioned at the outset, there is a very influential section of the society who think these arguments are phony and deliberately twisted to create an environment in favour of sport-hunting. Some of these people and arguments advanced by them against hunting of any kind are as follows:

1.   PeTA (People for Ethical Treatment of Animals) is a global animal rights NGO which promotes strict vegetarianism as a way of life and campaigns against all kinds of animal use, especially what it considers cruel practices. Under a caption aptly titled as "Why Sport Hunting Is Cruel and Unnecessary", it says that "Although it was a crucial part of humans" survival 100,000 years ago, hunting is now nothing more than a violent form of recreation that the vast majority of hunters do not need for subsistence. Hunting has contributed to the extinction of animal species all over the world, including the Tasmanian tiger and the great auk." According to PeTA, hunting is cruel and unnecessary because:

a. It causes pain and suffering to animals, especially as many animals and birds are injured but not bagged and such animals live or die in pain and hungry.

b. It disrupts migration and hibernation patterns and destroys families. For animals such as wolves, who mate for life and live in close-knit family units, hunting can devastate entire communities.

c. It is against the nature's way of regulation of populations because the predators kill the sick and the old while the trophy hunters want the best and the biggest, the animals needed to keep the populations strong.

d. Nature can regulate populations without human intervention through predation, disease and food supply.

e. Hunting leads to many shooting accidents.

f. The desire for profits leads the ranch owners to encourage malpractices such as canned hunts in which animals raised in captivity, and accustomed to human presence, are released in large enclosures for hunting, against the principle of "fair chase".

    Lastly, PeTA recommends that control of wild populations, if necessary, should be done through birth control (sterilisation, neutering, etc.) rather than through hunting.

2. Another organisation called The Animal Liberation Front (ALF) argues, under an essay

entitled as "The Fallacy of Sport Hunting" in America, that:

A growing number of Americans believe sport-hunting is unethical, wasteful, and unnecessary.

The number of hunters in the U.S. has declined over the past 20 years. (Note: This contention is not supported by the FWS report (FWS 2011) quoted previously in this chapter.)

A very small percentage of indigenous and rural hunters do kill animals as their main source of food. Most hunting today is done for "recreational" purposes – for the pure pleasure of pursuing and killing an animal.

Hunters often claim that hunting is a sport involving fair chase. However, a fair sport involves two individuals on equal grounds who have a mutual agreement to engage in the activity. It is hard to argue that an animal pursued by a hunter riding a snowmobile or off-road vehicle and equipped with high-powered firearms and electronic calling devices is on equal footing. State wildlife agencies often argue that our cities and rural lands would be overrun with wild animals if hunting were disallowed. However, the biological truth is that animals regulate their own populations, based upon available food and habitat.

Sport hunting does not result in an overall population decrease (of potentially dangerous and harmful animals) (Note: This contention is not supported by the data provided in IAFWA (2005) report).

Though our state wildlife agencies are mandated to protect wildlife and their habitats, their policies and regulations generally reflect a different agenda. The active promotion of sport-hunting and the perpetuation of "game species" over the interests of non-hunters and "non-game species" clearly indicates whose interests these agencies serve.

The more hunting licenses sold, the more funds a state receives from excise tax on guns, ammunition and hunting licenses due to Pittman-Robertson Act of 1937. States, therefore, have an incentive to cater to hunters over non-consumptive wildlife users because they will receive a larger slice of the federal funding pie.

3.   Another organisation called "In Defence of Animals (IDA)" uses exactly the same arguments as used by ALF, under a section called "Anti-Hunting" on its website (http://www.idausa.org/).

4.   "Wildlife Watch" is another global NGO that campaigns against sport-hunting through its "Committee Against Sport Hunting (C.A.S.H.)." Peter Muller (2007), writing in its newsletter using the data from the 2006 National Survey of Fishing, Hunting, and Wildlife-Associated Recreation (USFWS 2007), argues that "wildlife watching has now so decisively overtaken hunting by every measure that it is a "no-brainer" as to which activity should be encouraged and which should be phased out by the wildlife managing agencies."

He further argues that:

"Wildlife watching is incompatible with hunting. Abundance of wildlife attracts both wildlife watchers and hunters. The seasons when wildlife and migrating birds are of most interest to both hunters and wildlife watchers coincide. Wildlife watchers do not want to be afield in places when hunting takes place for an obvious concern for their own safety, as well as not wanting to witness the destruction of the fauna they have come to appreciate. It pretty much has to be one or the other, and any rational choice should be decisively in favor of wildlife watching. The comparison is given below:

Table 5: Comparative Economic Impact of Wildlife Watching and Hunting

Economic Parameter	Wildlife Watching	Hunting
No. of participants	71 mn	12.5 mn
% of population	31%	5%
Total expenditure	$40.5 bn	$21.3 bn
Expenses on food and lodges	$7.65 bn	$2.71 bn
Business status	Growing	Mature

Leaving all considerations of ethics aside, choosing simply to accommodate the preferred activity of the largest number of individuals who want to participate in wildlife-associated recreation – the choice has to be to favor wildlife watching over hunting. If we additionally consider the financial benefit to the community where the activity takes place – then there simply is no alternative except to opt for wildlife watching over hunting.

What about the impact on the ecosystem between wildlife watching and hunting? Here again, any objective, rational analysis will show that the ecosystem as a whole is much better served by wildlife watching than by hunting. The ecosystem is best served if biodiversity is naturally maintained. In order to accommodate hunting, wildlife managers will manipulate the habitat and promulgate regulations that permit the "maximum sustainable yield" or simply put the largest number of live targets for the hunters. That is akin to taking a forest that has a greatly diverse flora and turning it into a mono-crop plantation."

5. In February 2014, the U.S.A. imposed a complete ban on the commercial import of African ivory and limited the number of elephant trophies that can be imported by a hunter to two per year. No sport-hunted elephant trophies can be imported into the USA from Tanzania and Zimbabwe until the end of 2014 because "given the significant decline in the elephant population due to uncontrolled poaching and questionable management and governance, we are concerned

that additional killing of elephants, even if legal, is not sustainable and will not support effective elephant population recovery efforts in Tanzania."

(http://www.fws.gov/international/permits/by-activity/sport-hunted-trophies.html).

6. Commenting on the U.S. action, in the *National Geographic* blog called "A Voice for Elephants" on May 6, 2014 (Controversy Swirls Around the Recent U.S. Suspension of Sport-Hunted Elephant Trophies), Christina Russo, quoting several sources, gives the following arguments against sport-hunting of elephants in Africa:

a. According to International Fund for Animal Welfare (IFAW), the notion that sport-hunting helps conservation is a complete "sham". IFAW says that, "only about three percent of the hunting revenue actually goes to local community development" and "almost none of the money spent on expeditions accrues to local communities. Instead, it remains with the (mostly foreign) tour outfitters and travel companies, in urban centers, central government agencies and, often, bribes for officials."

b. Trophy hunting is in direct conflict with other activities that are truly sustainable, including wildlife viewing. People don't want to go to a landscape that has been hunted free of its animals.

c. The antipoaching effect of sport-hunting is sporadic and seasonal. "A lot of the time it's a one-man operation, and then they go back to town. They also leave at the end of the season when the rain starts and in fact, that's when a lot of our poaching happens."'

d. The big bulls, preferred by hunters, need to be protected as gene pool and objects of photography. "Once an elephant reaches a certain weight [of tusks], the animal should simply be considered "royal game," and [should be] completely untouchable. When you see those big old gentle tuskers, when they have lived that long, they should be given the protection they deserve."

e. The death of an elephant, especially the death of a female, has a severe impact on the survivors. The killing of a female is probably more devastating for other individual elephants because they live in tight knit families. When a female is killed, the repercussions can last a very long time. If the mother of a three- or four-year-old calf is killed, the calf will die. The survival rate of elephants even up to 20 years old is compromised if their mother is hunted. And if a matriarch is shot, it's absolutely devastating. It will have ramifications for years.

Although there are dozens of other organizations, and their websites, campaigning for and against sport hunting, arguments and counter arguments used by them are pretty much on standard lines, as described above. While these lobbies are fighting their battles, seeing victories and defeats in government actions and policies, the governments have to take decisions based on facts, not theories and sentiments. Thus, although the U.S.A. is not against sport hunting per se, as it declares in the order banning the import of elephant trophies from Tanzania that, "We recognize that sport-hunting as part of a sound management program, can provide benefits to wildlife conservation, and that sport-hunting of elephants is not the primary cause of the decline of elephant populations in Tanzania", it still placed restrictions on the import of African elephant trophies because the authorities believe that the conditions, like effective control on poaching and habitat protection, required to practice sustainable hunting may not be prevailing in Tanzania and Zimbabwe (http://www.fws.gov/international/pdf/non-detriment-finding-2014-elephant-Tanzania.pdf).

While the pro-hunting lobby sees this order as one based on misinformation, the anti-hunting lobby sees it as a vindication and acceptance of its position on hunting.

Botswana has, although temporarily, banned all hunting — except certain bird species — on all state and community lands beginning in 2014. Zambia cancelled all hunting licenses and concessions in 19 Game Management Areas for one year in January 2013. Besides, Zambia has also placed an indefinite ban on the hunting of lions and leopards. Both the decisions have been taken independently but for similar reasons, namely, uncontrolled poaching, habitat loss, declining populations and conflict with photographic tourism. While the anti-hunting groups are happy, though not entirely, at these developments (http://africainside.org/2014/02/10/botswana s-hunting-ban/), pro-hunting groups and tribal chiefs are aghast at these decisions.

"Chiefs in Nyimba (Zambia) have complained that the ban on issuance of hunting licenses has led to increased poaching activities in the district. .... some village scouts have resorted to poaching as opposed to protecting wildlife" (http://goo.gl/HRRtFd)

Comparison of Hunting and Non-Hunting Systems of Wildlife Management

Although the anti-hunting groups seem to believe that everything will be hunky dory if sport-hunting is banned, the examples of India and Kenya where there has been no hunting for nearly 40 years are not encouraging at all. In a "Comparison of national wildlife management strategies: What works, where and why?" Shalynn Pack *et al.* compare the North American, Southern African and No-Hunting (India and Kenya) wildlife management models in terms of their success in the fields of wildlife, economics and social benefits as shown in Fig. 1:

Fig. 1: Performance of Wildlife Management Models (Pack *et al.*)

Model	Country	Wildlife	Economics	Social Benefits	Protected Area Coverage	Sources
North American	USA	High	High	High	High	Organ et al. 2012
	Canada	High	Medium	High	High	
Southern African	South Africa	Medium	High	Medium	High	Reid et al. 2004
	Tanzania	Medium	High	High	High	
Non-Hunting	Kenya	Medium	Medium	Low	High	UNDP 2012
	India	Low	Low	Low	Low	Sanel 2004, Sekhar 2003

High   Medium   Low

Predictably, India fares the worst on all three counts, while Kenya fairs only slightly better, although both are at the bottom (Fig. 2).

Fig. 2: Comparison Among Models of Population Trends of Selected Large Mammal Species under Hunting and non-hunting wildlife Management Models (Pack *et al.*).

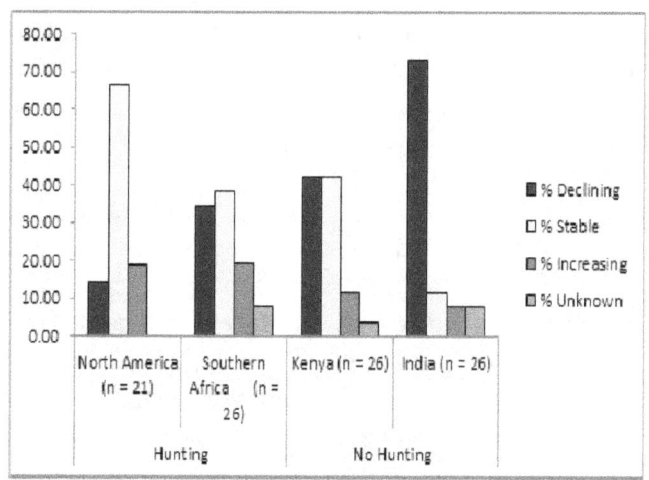

"n" is the number of species included in the analysis.

In conclusion, Pack *et al.* state that, "None of these wildlife management models is perfect, and each country faces a unique set of challenges to conserving its wildlife. Yet, comparing these countries' achievements in wildlife management, while acknowledging differences in context, offers a valuable lesson in "what works, where and why" for wildlife management strategies."

Synthesis of Pro-Hunting and Anti-Hunting Arguments

It is obvious that both the competing lobbies exaggerate their own contribution to conservation while disparaging the others'. Discounting the impractical thoughts that all killing and hunting is wrong, it is obvious that hunting tourism (sport-hunting) and non-hunting tourism can co-exist and complement each other in creating an economic value for wildlife and thus justifying conservation for the rich as well as for the poor. So, what are the bare facts in this cacophony of warring fanatics? Perhaps:

1.   Sport-hunting can exist only if poaching is under control. Although sport-hunting, like viewing tourism, reduces poaching, its direct antipoaching effect is very limited because hunters are generally very thinly spread and are there only for a short period of the year. However, if the local communities, who generally are the poachers, significantly benefit from hunting operations, they may voluntarily reduce poaching. Wildlife scouts funded by hunting revenues, where photographic tourism is not possible, may also help in reducing poaching.

2.   While photographic tourism happens in protected areas with high wildlife densities, sport-hunting generally happens outside PAs in areas with low wildlife densities, where photographic tourists would rarely like to go. Hence there should be no direct conflict between the two.

3.   It is true that the number of viewing tourists in the world is much more than hunters. Consequently, the economic activity generated by tourists is much more than that generated by

hunters, although hunters spend much more money per person than other tourists. Both these contributions are important and non-negligible and conservation will suffer in the absence of either of them, especially where these funds go for conservation work and for supporting the rural communities.

4. All tourists are not hunters, but all hunters and anglers go to parks for photography and ecotourism. Even for inveterate hunters, hunting trips are few and far between while visits to parks are far more frequent. Hence if sport-hunting is banned, perhaps they will increase their visits to parks. In that case, the parks will benefit but the remote communities and their wildlife will lose the benefit of their visits.

5. Killing of animals is going to happen as long as there is wildlife. In some cases, animals may have to be killed for management purposes, while in other cases they may be killed for food or other goods. In the absence of legal hunting, animals will be killed by poachers and in much larger numbers. Hunting by tourists can generate much more economic value per animal for local people than hunting the same number of animals by the people themselves. As sport hunters are interested only in the trophy, the meat generally goes (or can go) to the local communities. This, perhaps, douses their desire to hunt for food to that extent.

6. It is likely to be true that most of the economic value created by hunting is captured by the big

commercial interests and the locals benefit only from the minimal trickledown effect. However, even the minimal benefits in terms of jobs created for the local people may still be quite significant in many cases, due to the absence of any other economic opportunities in remote areas.

7.   Even if hunting may create considerable economic value for the local communities, at least in some areas, income to the individual households — if there is any income distribution at all — is generally insignificant, except to those who are able to garner jobs. In most cases, this income stays with the community bodies or their federations and is used for infrastructure development rather than for supporting households.

8.   Trophy hunting is unlikely to be an effective tool for controlling problem populations, as the trophy animals, i.e. big males, are generally a very small part of a population. If the hunters go only for over-mature, non-breeding males, as they always claim, then the regulatory effect will be even more insignificant. More drastic measures, such as culling or killing of breeding females, may be required to control the growth of a problem population.

9.   Sport-hunting is likely to have some adverse effect on the genetics of the hunted populations as there is a possibility of lesser males getting an opportunity to breed when a dominant male, with a good trophy value, is picked up by a hunter. It

may not be true that all trophy animals are beyond their breeding age. However, as most species are polygamous and promiscuous, and most males have no significant role in breeding, the effect of removal of a few males from a population may not be very significant.

10.   In most species, males have no role in bringing up their young, and may move from one herd to another in search of receptive females. Therefore, the death of a trophy male may not have any deleterious effect on the survival of the young or the social structure of species. However, the death of a female with young off spring, especially in species with strong social bonds such as elephants, will certainly affect the well-being of the young. Sport-hunting is no substitute for natural selection. It is true that in nature the predators tend to catch the old, sick or weak animals, and thus keep the populations healthy. In contrast, trophy hunters tend to kill the fittest animals first. However, the removal of a few trophy males, which are generally surplus in a population and perhaps a burden on resources, should not seriously affect the general health of the population.

11.   It seems an oversimplification that nature can take care of the population management issues if left to itself. No predators are likely to be able to control elephant populations if there are too many. Nature will reduce their population only when they have destroyed and degraded their habitat to a point that they are unable to feed

themselves. But in the meantime, they will wreak havoc on the nearby communities and may endanger or wipe out some other species by destroying their common habitat. Perhaps for maintaining maximum biodiversity and to protect human life and property, managers or hunters have to step in and control populations. Without human protection against more successful competitors or predators, some species may just be wiped out.

12. Ethics and morality is a difficult subject to discuss as it is very individualistic and personal. What is right for one is completely unacceptable to the other. To the animal rights advocates, all killing is unethical. To some hunters, only certain kinds of killing (say canned hunting, lack of fair chase) is unethical, while to others nothing is unethical. If we accept the views of the animal rights groups, human existence will be almost impossible as there can just be no life without eating other organisms. The contention of the hunters that their killing, even under true fair chase conditions, is ethical also seems self-serving, as there just cannot be any fair competition between humans, with all the equipment at their disposal, and animals, with only instincts to depend on. Hunters should admit that they cannot claim any higher moral ground just on the basis of claims of so-called "fair chase," and must justify their pursuits on grounds of benefit to human society and environment.

13. Hunting, like any other enterprise, needs to be strictly regulated and controlled. In the absence of strict regulation, the chances of unscrupulous hunters exceeding their quota limits and specifications, going beyond their allocated area in search or pursuit of a trophy, leaving an injured animal in pain, or endangering human beings will always be there. Problems in Tanzania and Zimbabwe, etc. seem to be more of governance rather than sport-hunting itself.

Although the moral stances of both the parties are beyond reconciliation, the above synthesis of pro- and anti-hunting arguments clearly indicates that sport-hunting can be a strong tool for conservation and rural development under the following conditions:

(a) There is no, or minimal, poaching or killing beyond the sustainable quotas determined on a scientific basis.

(b) Significant economic benefits accrue to the communities traditionally dependent upon these resources. Apart from giving them full rights over trophy fees, they may also be encouraged to provide support services like hospitality, transport, etc. to the clients. As most of the poaching is done by the local people, success in (b) can ensure success in (a) as well.

(c) Hunters and their organisations must ensure strict compliance with quotas and regulations and any violations must invite stringent penalties.

In fact (a) and (b) are the essence of modern conservation and any strategy that promises progress on this road deserves to be seriously examined.

Scope for Conservation Hunting in India

In the light of the preceding discussion, which clearly brings out the value of community-based sport-hunting programmes in conservation in Africa, it is interesting to examine how this strategy can be applied in India.

WLPA had a complete set of provisions for sport-hunting of wild animals when it was promulgated in 1972. Sections 9 to 17 regulated hunting and sections 39 to 49 provided for regulation of trade and transfer of wildlife specimens. However, most of these provisions were either deleted or modified over time in order to outlaw sport hunting. In its current form, hunting is allowed only in case of animals becoming dangerous to human life or property (sec. 11), for scientific research and education (section 12), and "for the improvement and better management of wild life" in protected areas {sec. 29 and 35 (6)}. The law does not allow the killing of animals for "scientific management" (sec. 12), but one can "destroy, exploit or remove wild life" "for the improvement and better management of wild life" in PAs {sec. 29 and 35 (6)}. All animals so killed, and their trophies and derivatives, are government property (sec 11 and sec. 39). Many states, such as MP, UP, Uttarkhand, Rajasthan Maharashtra, Andhra Pradesh, Telangana, Punjab and Haryana, allow hunting of wild pig and blue bull under a permit under section 11 but do not allow the consumption of meat of the hunted animals, i.e. the carcass has to be burnt or buried. Section 44 permits trade in wild animals and their products, but section 43 and 49 prohibit all trade in species listed in schedule I and part II of schedule II. Wading through this maze of conflicting provisions, one concludes that, despite the clear intention of the law not to allow any sport-hunting, species belonging to schedules other than schedule I and part II of schedule II can still be subjected to conservation hunting and trade, thanks to the incompetence of the people who wrote and approved all the amendments to the original Act. However, only an adventurous state will dare to do it. MP came quite close to doing it several times, as long as I was there to push them, but could not go the whole hog, not because they were worried about the law, but because the politicians and bureaucrats could not muster the courage to do something unconventional. It is unlikely that any state will think of doing it now. Instead of finding ways of converting surplus wild animals into an economic resource, Although GoI has now started allowing the killing of wild pig, *nilgai*, and rhesus macaque, as vermin (under section 62 of the Act) outside forests, on the request of the states, here too the states have to spend exorbitant amounts on contract killers, rather than converting disposable animals into an economic resource by selling hunting licenses.

In the context of the above legal position, it is obvious that this discussion is only of an academic nature as, even if a viable template emerges from this narrative, it cannot be implemented properly without amending the law, which takes decades to happen. Amending the law to allow hunting will be even more difficult in view of its controversial nature and its potential to raise the sentimental hackles across the world.

Secondly, as India is a huge and diverse country, the template discussed below may not apply uniformly to all situations. Therefore, even if hunting becomes an acceptable solution to India's conservation problems someday, several variations of a prototype will have to be worked out to fit each situation squarely.

A hypothetical conservation-hunting programme in India shall follow the following template:

- There shall be no hunting inside protected areas unless some special situation so requires. For example, if the management wants to reduce the population of a species which is either harming the habitat or is becoming an intolerable problem for the neighbourhood, sport-hunting can be one of the options. In general, the role of the PAs will be to act as the breeding centres to allow surplus animals to spill over into the neighbouring forests where they can be subjected to hunting regulations.

- Hunting can be practiced only if the management agencies understand the wildlife populations completely. They need to know the population size, male-female ratio, birth rate, growth rate, etc. reliably to be able to work out the annual off take correctly. For this to happen, wildlife biologists will be required to monitor the target populations continuously. Standard procedures and protocols shall have to be prescribed for monitoring and evaluating populations and their vital rates. It may not be farfetched to expect that local management staff is able to identify the huntable animals individually, as the number of animals to be hunted, at least in the beginning, shall be very small.

- Hunting cannot be considered as a management option if an effective control on poaching is not possible. Therefore, the government agencies and the partner communities have to be certain that they will be able to control poaching before going ahead with a hunting programme. People can argue that when the populations are small, why start a hunting programme. Sport hunting is a support to populations dwindling under poaching pressure. Successful hunting programmes in Namibia, Pakistan and many other countries were started when the wildlife populations were very small, but they recovered significantly under the influence of these programmes as poaching levels went down.

- By and large, especially in the beginning, the programme shall focus on ungulate species only, as the density of carnivores outside protected areas is negligible and it will be prudent that no breeding carnivore is killed even by mistake. However, if carnivore populations are reliably known to be good, and a problem like the leopard in some parts of the Garhwal Himalayas, sport-hunting can be one of the strategies to manage the population.

- Ungulate populations available for hunting can be divided into two categories. First category is the animals living inside notified forests. We would like these populations to grow despite the hunting. These populations can be subjected to the "trophy-hunting" version of hunting in which only a few old and mature males are hunted. Second category of candidate populations will be the species, like blue bull, blackbuck, wild boar, etc., living in and around agricultural lands and which destroy crops. Here the objective of hunting can be to reduce or stabilise these populations to keep crop losses within tolerable limits. In such situations, the hunting quotas can be higher and even females can be allowed to be hunted.

- At present, neither the forest departments have any experience in managing hunting operations nor do the Indian hunters have the expertise in tracking and bagging wild animals. Current practices of poaching are stealth operations, without any rules and restrictions. Therefore, the forest departments, local guides and support staff, as well as the potential hunters, shall have to be adequately educated and trained in their respective crafts before they can be charged with any responsibility related to hunting. Adequate training facilities, perhaps with foreign trainers, will have to be created sufficiently before the first animal is shot.

- The programme has to benefit communities significantly in order to be of any use to conservation. As there are virtually no "community lands" in most of India (except the North-East), as in Africa, we have to find a basis for the involvement of communities in the programme. One solution can be to use the joint forest management (JFM) programmes, prevalent in all states, as the vehicle to create space for community involvement. Most forest areas in the country have been allotted to various village communities for the purpose of joint management. The areas allocated to each village can become the basis and measure of their share in the programme.

- As the "hunting blocks" will have to be larger than the areas of individual communities, several communities can come together to form a federation to pool their areas to create a viable hunting block. As a thumb rule, one hunting block may be approximately the size of one sub-range (approx. 3000 ha) and may be sub-divided into sections, depending on physical markers. The hunting block may include the adjoining agricultural land, although crop lands can be made independent hunting blocks as the management objectives in these areas shall be different from the forest blocks. Representatives from all the JFM committees situated in the block can nominate their representatives to form a "Wildlife Management Committee" for the block. This committee shall coordinate with the forest department in developing and managing the hunting programme and distributing the income to member communities.

- A system has to be devised to get the best returns from a limited harvest of a block through proper marketing. Neither the forest department nor communities are likely to be good at it. One option can be that the hunting rights in the block are sold to an agent through an open and transparent auction or tendering system. The agent can then retail hunting permits to Indians and foreigners. The agent will be responsible for providing the necessary logistic support to the hunters as well as for ensuring that all the rules and regulations are followed scrupulously. This will save the forest staff the burden of supervising individual hunters, and will bring in private expertise and capital. If the agent is also given the permission to run ecotourism operations in the area in the non-hunting season, it can generate additional income for the agent, a share in which can be negotiated for the community.

- Annual off take shall be determined by competent biologists on the basis of the status of the population and its various vital rates. The off take shall depend upon whether the population is growing or shrinking, especially on the proportion of males in the population. The off take is likely to be only 2-5% of the estimated population, and only old males, unless a higher off take is allowed in order to reduce crop damage or any other losses.

- All the income from the trophy fee (paid by the agent or individual hunters) shall directly go to the account of the "wildlife management committee". There are unlikely to be any significant expenses on the programme, except the tendering process. Of course there will be expenses on consultancies and training programmes, which can be easily borne by the government. The committee shall be free to decide how to use this income, in consultation with, and approval of, the communities constituting the committee.

- The government may start a system of issuing "hunting licenses" to persons who are interested in hunting in the state. This license should be issued only to a person who knows the basic jungle craft, gun handling and safety procedures. As there is no hunting culture in the country, we may consider making some kind of training mandatory for acquiring the license. This training may not be necessary in the case of persons who may have hunted abroad. The government can charge a fee for issuing the license. Only licensed hunters shall be allowed to buy a hunting permit.

- If we allow hunting, we will also have to create regulations on how meat, skins and trophies shall be handled, traded or transferred. In a true trophy hunting operation, a hunter is allowed to take only 3-5 kg of meat while the rest is delivered to a designated butcher who disposes it on behalf of the community. However, for local hunters meat may be as important as the trophy itself. As no hunter is likely to be able to consume all the meat himself, the regulations will have to provide a framework for dealing with the surpluses.

- The Arms Act 1959 and related rules shall have to be reviewed in order to make the import, export and temporary possession of weapons possible by local and foreign hunters.

- Detailed hunting rules, particularly focusing on hunter behaviour in the forests, shall have to be developed. Chapter III of the Wildlife (Protection) Act, 1972, as originally enacted, provided the basic legal framework for practicing sport-hunting, although a ban on hunting was also imposed almost simultaneously. These sections were later deleted or amended to outlaw sport-hunting completely. Different countries have varying regulation regimes for hunting, but they all promote the true hunting spirit by making hunting a tough outdoors adventure and provide safeguards for the animals against excessive killing, cruelty and pain. Even the WLPA, as originally drafted nearly 40 years ago, was heavily loaded in favour of animals rather than hunters. Section 17 of the Act, before deletion, had provided as shown below:

17. (1) No person shall –

 (a) hunt any wild animal, from or by means of, a wheeled or a

1.   mechanically propelled vehicle, on water, or land, or by aircraft;

2.   use an aircraft, motor vehicle or launch for the purpose of driving or stampeding any wild animal;

(b)   hunt any wild animal with chemicals, explosives, nets, pitfalls, poisons, poisoned weapons, snares or traps, except in so far as they relate to the capture of wild animals under a Wild Animal Trapping Licence;

(c)   hunt any special game or big game other than with a rifle, unless specially authorised by the licence to hunt with a shot-gun using single-slug bullets;

(d)   for the purpose of hunting, set fire to any vegetation;

(e)   use any artificial light for the purpose of hunting, except when specially authorised to do so under a licence in the case of carnivore over a kill;

(f)   hunt any wild animal during the hours of night, that is to say, between sun-set and sun-rise, except when specially authorised to do so under a licence in the case of carnivore over a kill

(g)   hunt any wild animal on a salt lick or water hole or other drinking place or on path or approach to the same, except sand-grouse and water-birds;

(h)   hunt any wild animal on any land not owned by Government, without the consent of the owner or his agent or the lawful occupier of such land;

(i)   notwithstanding that he holds a licence for the purpose, hunt any wild animal during the closed time referred to in section 16;

(j)   hunt, with the help of dogs, any wild animal except water-bird, chakor, partridge or quail.

(2)   The provisions of sub-section (1) shall not apply to vermin.

These provisions can be revised in the light of international best practices to ensure that we are able to generate maximum benefits for wildlife and communities.

Conclusion

It is obvious from the above discussion that community-based sport-hunting as a conservation tool deserves serious consideration in developing countries where local communities as well as commercial smugglers are overexploiting the wildlife resources. In the USA, sport-hunting may be relevant for conservation because hunters' taxes finance the conservation agencies, besides limiting wildlife damages. But in Asia and Africa, where rural communities still follow traditional resource-dependent lifestyles, it has an added relevance as a tool for reducing this overexploitation, besides strengthening sustainability of rural livelihoods.

Having been trained and nurtured in the preservation of wildlife, on the same principles as most of the anti-hunting people of the world, I will, personally, never have the guts or desire to go out and kill an animal for fun or food. However, I also do not have the temerity to have a closed mind to an idea which seems to possess the potential to achieve the improbable – success in conservation of wildlife.

As they say, it is never too late. Perhaps someday, someone in India will have the courage to test the waters, of course, cautiously. We never thought tigers, especially captive bred, could be reintroduced in the wild. People thought we were foolhardy when we dared to return the gaur to Bandhavgarh fifteen years after its local extinction. Now both these fancies are a reality. Who knows? Someday we may have one more new reality!!

Notes

1. Until the recent land reforms programme derailed the well-known CAMPFIRE programme. (http://www.zimbabwesituation.com/news/zim sit_poaching-threatens-campfire-programme/)

2. Violation of NTCA's directions regarding tiger conservation by any "person, officer or authority" in India is an offence as per section 38 O (2) of the Wild Life (Protection) Act 1972 and offending government officials can go to jail for violating these advisories.

3. Although community-based natural resource management (CBNRM) initiatives have generally been successful, so far, in reversing the trend in declining wildlife populations, their long term viability is questionable due to the primary reason that most of the income accruing to the communities is spent on common causes and accruals to individual households are very small. Moreover, communities get only a very small proportion of the gross income as most of it goes to the government in the form of fees and taxes, and to the safari operators (mainly white) in the form of operating expenses and profits. Their current apparent sustainability is also a result of donor funding, which such programmes readily attract.

Bibliography

1. Ahmed Javed, Naseer Tareen, and Paind Khan, 2003: *Conservation of Sulaiman Markhor and Afghan Urial by Local Tribesmen in Torghar, Pakistan*: IUCN: Lessons Learned: Case Studies in Sustainable Use, 2001

2. Aiyadurai Ambika (2007): Hunting in a Biodiversity Hotspot: A survey on hunting practices by indigenous communities in Arunachal Pradesh, North-east India. Nature Conservation Foundation (NCF).

3. Ali, Sajjad, 2008: Conservation and Status of *Markhor* (Capra falconeri) in the Northern Parts of North West Frontier Province, Pakistan. Professional Paper for MS Wildlife Biology, University of Montana, Misoula, USA.

4. Animal Use Affairs Committee of International Association of Fish and Wildlife Agencies (IAFWA) 2005: *Potential Costs of Losing Hunting and Trapping as Wildlife Management Methods.*

5. Animal Use Issues Committee of the International Association of Fish and Wildlife Agencies (*IAFWA*) 2004: *Potential Costs of Losing Hunting and Trapping as Wildlife Management Tools.*

6. Arthshastra: (http://en.wikipedia.org/wiki/Arthashastra#Wildlife_and_forests)

7. Ashley Caroline, Charlotte Boyd and Harold Goodwin 2000: PRO-POOR TOURISM: *Putting Poverty At The Heart Of The Tourism Agenda*; ODI, Natural Resource Perspectives Number 51, March 2000.

8. Barnes, J.I. and de Jager, J.L.V. 1996. Economic and financial incentives for wildlife use on private land in

Bibliography

Namibia and the implications for policy. South African Journal of Wildlife Research 26(2): 37-46.

9. Bharatratna Dr. P.V. Kane: *Dharamshastra Ka Itihas*

10. Bitapi C. Sinha, Qamar Qureshi, V. K. Uniyal & S. Sen (): Economics *of wildlife tourism – contribution to livelihoods of communities around Kanha tiger reserve, India,* Journal of Ecotourism, DOI:10.10 80/14724049.2012.721785

11. BOOKBINDER MARNIE P., ERIC DINERSTEIN, ARUN RIJAL, HANK CAULEY, AND ARUP RAJOURIA 1998: *Ecotourism's Support of Biodiversity Conservation;* Conservation Biology, Pages 1399–1404 Volume 12, No. 6, December 1998.

12. Buckley Ralf C. and H. S. Pabla, 2012: *Tourism ban won't help Indian tigers.* Nature, Sept. 6, 2012.

13. Buckley, R. and Sommer, M. (2001). *Tourism and Protected Areas: Partnerships in Principle and Practice.* CRC for Sustainable Tourism Pty Ltd. and Tourism Council Australia, Sydney, Australia.

14. Ceballos-Lascurain Hector 1992-*Tourism, ecotourism, and* protected *areas,* IV World Congress on National Parks and Protected Areas, IUCN, Gland, Switzerland

15. Ceballos-Lascuráin, Héctor. 1992. Tourism, Ecotourism, and Protected Areas. IV World Congress on National Parks and Protected Areas, IUCN, Gland, Switzerland..

16. Ceballos-Lascurain, Hector. 1993. *IUCN Ecotourism Consultancy.*

17. CHUTIA P. & G. S. SOLANKI (2003): Patterns of bird hunting in Arunachal Pradesh and implications for biodiversity conservation, Tropical Ecology 54(2): 263-267.

18. Daniel Stynes Daniel, Dennis Propst, and Ya-Yen Sun, 2001: *Economic Impacts of Visitors to Olympic National Park, 2000.* Michigan State University.

19. DeGeorges Paul Andre and Brian Kevin Reilly 2009: The Realities of Community Based Natural Resource Management and Biodiversity Conservation in Sub-Saharan Africa. Sustainability. 1, 734-788.

20. DeGeorges, Paul Andre, 1992. ADMADE: *An Evaluation, Today And The Future, Policy Issues And Direction.* United States Agency For International Development and The National Parks And Wildlife Service Of Zambia.

21. Dhammika, Ven. S. 1993: *The Edicts of King Asoka.* Buddhist Publication Society, Kandy, Sri Lanka.

22. Edwards, Stephen R. 2006. *Saving Biodiversity for Human Lives in Northern Pakistan.* Mountain Areas Conservancy Project. The World Conservation Union (IUCN), Pakistan Country Office, Karachi, Pakistan. 38 pp.

23. Elwin, Verrier (1939): The Baiga. Gyan Publishing House, New Delhi (Reprint 2002).

24. Fillion *et al.* 1992: Fillion, Fern L., Foley, James P., and Jacquemot, André J. (1992) *The Economics of Global Ecotourism.* Paper presented at the Fourth World Congress on National Parks and Protected Areas, Caracas, Venezuela, February10-21, 1992.

25. Forsyth J. Captain (1871): Highlands of Central India, Natraj Publishers, Dehra Dun (Reprint 1994).

26. Gadgil Madhav and Romila Thapar; quoted by Aloka Parashar-Sen in the *Environmental History of India,* edited by Mahesh Rangarajan and K. Sivaramakrishnan).

27. Higginbottom K, Chelsea Northrope and Ronda Green 2001: *Positive Effects Of Wildlife Tourism On Wildlife;* CRC for Sustainable Tourism, ISBN 1 876685 37 9.

Bibliography

28. High Court of MP, Jabalpur, order dated 1.11.2002, 4.8.2003 and 12.11.2003, WP no. 5937/2002 (AVM DS Mishra VS. State of MP).

29. Hilaluddin, R. Kaul & D. Ghose, (2005): Conservation implications of wild animal biomass extractions in Northeast India. Animal Biodiversity and Conservation.

30. Iverson, S.J. (1982). *Breeding White Tigers Zoogoer* 11:5–12.

31. Jhala Y.V., R.Gopal, Q. Qureshi (eds.) (2008). *Status of the Tigers, Co-predators, and Prey in India.* National Tiger Conservation Authority, Govt. of India, New Delhi, and Wildlife Institute of India, Dehradun.

32. Jon Rosen 2010: *Rwanda: where there are baby gorillas to* name. Tourism and community involvement helps endangered mountain gorillas beat survival odds, globalpost june 28, 2010.

33. Kala Arvind: *The Flesh-Eaters of India*: Times of India, Oct. 25, 2005

34. Karanth K. Ullas, Raghunandan Singh Chundawat, James D. Nichol and N Samba Kumar, 2004: Estimation of tiger densities in the tropical dry forests of Panna, Central India, using photographic capture–recapture sampling. Animal Conservation (2004) 7, 285–290.The Zoological Society of London.

35. Karanth KK, Gopalaswamy AM, DeFries R, Ballal N (2012) Assessing Patterns of Human-Wildlife Conflicts and Compensation around a Central Indian Protected Area. PLoS ONE 7(12): e50433. doi:10.1371/journal.pone.0050433

36. Karanth Ullas, John Goodrich, Srinivas Vaidyanathan (Wildlife Conservation Society, 2004): *Tigers and their prey: Predicting carnivore densities from prey abundance.* University of Washington, Seattle.

37. Karanth, K. K. and DeFries, R. (2010). *Nature-based tourism in Indian protected areas: New challenges for park management.* Conservation Letters 4: 137-149. DOI: 10.1111/j.1755-263X.2010.00154.x.

38. Karki J. B. and Thapa B. B. 2011: *Status of blue sheep and Himalayan tahr in Dhorpatan Hunting Reserve, Nepal.* BANKO JANAKARI (A JOURNAL OF FORESTRY INFORMATION FOR NEPAL), Vol21, No. 1. May 2011.

39. Kreuter U. Peel Mike and Edward Warner, 2010: Wildlife Conservation and Community-Based Natural Resource Management in Southern Africa's Private Nature Reserves: Society and Natural Resources, 23:507–524.

40. KRITHI K. KARANTH, RUTHDEFRIES, ARJUN SRIVATHSA and VISHNUPRIYA SANKARAMAN, 2012: *Wildlife tourists in India's emerging economy: potential for a conservation constituency?* Fauna & Flora International, Oryx, 1–9.

41. Leopold Aldo: *History of Ideas*: Game Management

42. Lewis DM, Mwenya A. and Kaweche G.B. (undated): African Solutions to Wildlife Problems in Africa: Insights from a Community-Based Project in Zambia. FAO CORPORATE DOCUMENT REPOSITORY.

43. Madhusudan M.D., Karanth K. Ullas (2002): Hunting for an Answer: Is Local Hunting Compatible with Large Mammal Conservation in India Ambio, Feb 2002.

44. Mahabharata: Mrigswapanodbhavaparva (Deer/antelope in Dreams), *Van Parv* - Chapter 257

45. Muller Peter, Peter 2007: *Wildlife watching: an economic boon to communities:* The C.A.S.H. Courier, 2007 Fall issue.

46. Munn, Ian A. Anwar Hussain, Stan Spurlock and James E. Henderson, 2010: Economic Impact of Fishing, Hunting and Wildlife-Associated Recreation Related Expenditures on the Southeastern U.S. Regional

Bibliography

Economy: An Input-Output Analysis: Human Dimension of Wildlife 15:433-449, 2010.

47. NSSO Press Note dated 30 April, 2007

48. NTCA (National Tiger Conservation Authority) 2012: Comprehensive Guidelines for tiger conservation and tourism as provided under section 38 O (1) (c) of the Wild Life (Protection) Act, 1972, PART-B: GUIDELINES FOR TOURISM IN AND AROUND TIGER RESERVES. Circular dated 15 October, 2012.

49. Pabla H. S. 1997: *Conflict Around Protected Areas.* - Vacham, April 1997. Bhopal, India.

50. Pabla H. S. 2005: *'Use It Or Lose It': The Mantra For Man-Animal Co-Existence;* Paper Presented at the International Seminar on Man Animal Co-existence, Kaziranga National Park, India, February. 15, 2005.

51. PACEC 2006: Shooting Sports – findings of an economic and environmental and survey, Public and Corporate Economic Consultants (PACEC).

52. Pack Shalynn, Rachel Golden, Ashlee Walker, Martha Surridge, Jonathan Mawdsley: Comparison of national wildlife management strategies: What works where and why? Wildlife Consulting Associates, Heinz Center for Science, Economics and Environment, University of Maryland.

53. Prerna Singh Bindra: Report on impact of tourism on tigers and other wildlife in Corbett Tiger Reserve: A study for the Ministry of Tourism, Government of India.

54. Rajagopalachari C: *RAMAYANA Retold.* Edited by Jay Mazo, American Gita Society.

55. Rangarajan Mahesh 2001: India's Wildlife History. Published by Permanent Black, New Delhi.

56. Richardson, J.A. 1998. Wildlife utilization and biodiversity conservation in Namibia: conflicting or

complementary objectives? Biodiversity and Conservation 7: 549-559.

57. Saayman M., P. van der Merwe and R Rossouw, 2005: *The impact of hunting for biltong purposes on the SA economy.* North West University, South Africa.

58. Sun Ya-Yen,, Daniel J. Stynes, and Dennis B. Propst, 2002: *Economic Impacts of Visitors to Mount Rainier National Park, 2000.* Michigan State University.

59. U.S. Department of the Interior, U.S. Fish and Wildlife Service, and U.S. Department of Commerce, U.S. Census Bureau. *2011 National Survey of Fishing, Hunting, and Wildlife-Associated Recreation.*

60. US Department of the Interior, US Fish and Wildlife Service, and U.S. Department of Commerce, U.S. Census Bureau, 2014: *2011 National Survey of Fishing, Hunting and Wildlife-Associated Recreation.*

61. US Department of the Interior, US Fish and Wildlife Service, and U.S. Department of Commerce, U.S. Census Bureau, *2007: National Survey of Fishing, Hunting and Wildlife-Associated Recreation.*

62. Weaver, Larrye Chris And Patricia Skyer, 2003: Conservancies: Integrating Wildlife Land-Use Options Into The Livelihood, Development, And Conservation Strategies Of Namibian Communities; A Paper Presented At The Vth World Parks Congress Durban, Republic Of South Africa, September 8-17, 2003.

63. Western David, Michael Wright; Shirley Strum, Ed. *1994: Zimbabwe"s Communal Areas Management Programme for Indigenous Resources.* Natural Connections: Perspectives in Community-based Conservation. Island Press. Washington D.C.

64. Wildlife Watching and Tourism: A study on the benefits and risks of a fast growing tourism activity and its impacts on species. UNEP/CMS Secretariat, Bonn, Germany. 68 pages.

Bibliography

65. Woodford MH, M.R. FRISINA, G.A. AWAN (undated): Veterinary concerns for the Management of the Suleiman *Markhor* (Capra *falconeri megaceros*) and the Afghan Urial (Ovis *orientalis cycloceros*) in the Torghar Hills, Balochistan, Pakistan.

66. World Tourism Organisation 2002: *Tourism and Poverty Alleviation.*

67. World Tourism Organization (2012), Annual Report 2011, UNWTO, Madrid

68. World Travel and Tourism Council (WTTC) 2013: Benchmarking Travel and Tourism in India, How does Travel and Tourism compare to other sectors? Summary of findings 2013.

69. World Travel and Tourism Council (WTTC) 2013: Benchmarking Travel and Tourism in India, How does Travel and Tourism compare to other sectors? Summary of findings 2013.

About the Author

Dr. Harbhajan Singh Pabla grew up in a Punjabi village, in India. He joined the Indian Forest Service in 1977 and retired as the Chief Wildlife Warden of the state of Madhya Pradesh in February 2012. Apart from doing the usual things that an Indian forester does, he nurtured his love for the wilds while managing national parks like Kanha, Panna and Bandhavgarh. Along the way, he developed a penchant for questioning the status quo and challenged the stereotypes that have ruled the conservation mindset in the country. He introduced the concept of "conservation by incentive" in the form of a cash reward to farmers for hosting an endangered bird, the lesser florican, in their croplands. He was responsible for changing the face of wildlife tourism in Madhya Pradesh, despite opposition from NTCA, and made tourism revenue a significant resource in tiger reserves of the state. When Panna lost all its tigers, he developed and implemented the tiger reintroduction plan that has given the world the confidence that wild tigers will always be around. He was the principal force behind the reintroduction of gaur in Bandhavgarh and blackbuck in Kanha, after both the species had become locally extinct in the nineties. His unfinished agenda for the state included the reintroduction of barasingha in the Forsyth country, i.e. the Satpura Tiger Reserve, and the white tiger in its native Sanjay Tiger Reserve. Barasingha has already reached Bori in Satpura, and he hopes to see white tigers in the wild before saying adieu to this world. He unsuccessfully tried to introduce community-based sport-hunting for the conservation of crop raiding species. His wish-list for conservation also includes seeing Indian foresters riding horses for patrolling and enjoying the wilderness.

Apart from a stint on the faculty of the Wildlife Institute of India, he has been an international consultant in wildlife management.

He is an ardent tennis player and lives in Bhopal, India. He can be contacted at:

E-mail: pablahsifs@gmail.com

Phone: +91-9425007850, +91-755-2980026.

Reader Reviews